A WORLD IN TRAVAIL

A World in Travail

A Study of the Contemporary World Crisis

T. B. MASTON

Professor of Social Ethics
Southwestern Baptist Theological Seminary
Fort Worth, Texas

BROADMAN PRESS

Nashville, Tennessee

Printed in the United States of America
5.053KSP

To

THE STUDENTS

Who have shared with me
in the study of

THE WORLD CRISIS

CONTENTS

Foreword: I. *Brooks Hays*   ix
          II. *Joseph M. Dawson*
Preface   xiii

  I. *Evidences of the Crisis*   1
       CONDITIONS WITHIN OUR NATION
       THE GENERAL WORLD SITUATION
       THE CONTEMPORARY FRAME OF MIND
       MODERN WORLD MOVEMENTS
       THE VERDICT OF THE SCHOLARS

 II. *Background of the Crisis*   24
       SOURCES OF WESTERN CIVILIZATION
       THE EARLY CHRISTIAN CENTURIES
       THE UNIFICATION OF CIVILIZATION
       FRAGMENTATION OF CIVILIZATION
       SUBSEQUENT DEVELOPMENTS
       THE CONTEMPORARY SCENE

III. *Phases of the Crisis*   44
       THE ECONOMIC
       THE POLITICAL
       THE RELIGIOUS

 IV. *Factors in the Crisis*   66
       WARS AND RUMORS OF WARS

SHIFTING POWER POSITIONS
SCIENCE AND THE MACHINE AGE
THE MARCH OF THE MASSES
DECADENCE OF MORAL FOUNDATIONS

V. *Heart of the Crisis*   89
DISINTEGRATION OF INTEGRATING CENTER
SECULARIZATION OF LIFE
DETHRONEMENT OF GOD
LOSS OF FAITH

VI. *Cure for the Crisis*   113
PRELIMINARY QUESTIONS
RETURN TO GOD
RENEWAL OF ORGANIZED CHRISTIANITY
INTERVENTION OF GOD

VII. *A Personal Program*   137

FOREWORD

A MUTUAL interest in the social service activities of our denomination is responsible for my friendship with the author, and I have developed a deep appreciation of his ability to appraise social issues and to suggest practical means of applying the Christian gospel to the problems of contemporary life.

In *A World in Travail* Dr. Maston highlights our indebtedness to Europe for a cultural heritage that found its rich fruition in Christian civilization, but he properly suggests humility in pointing to present world tensions. These tensions result, he believes, largely from our failure to project Christian ideals into all the areas of life into which our commercial, political, and military operations have carried us. In other words, in attributing some of our present tensions to the exposure of peoples of the Orient, previously unacquainted with Western culture, to our ideals and our imperfections, he lays the basis for an important thesis.

Dr. Maston's thesis that there is a world crisis, that this crisis does have enormous significance, and that it must be defined in spiritual terms if the new structure for world society is to have enduring foundations, is forcefully developed. The appeal of his message to Christian people to take note of the fact of the interdependence of all nations is convincing. His presentation of the urgency of the crisis and his insistence that we as Christians have a distinctive contribution to make to the resolving of unprecedented conflicts and struggles represent a valuable addition to our literature.

BROOKS HAYS

House of Representatives
Washington, D. C.

II

One of the best informed creative thinkers among the theological seminary professors of our day has in these readable pages concentrated upon our sick society. He feels that the stricken world has reached a point in the maladies from which it suffers that may well be regarded as extremely critical. Whatever the cause of our sick society, the crisis is far from imaginary. Upon the contrary, it is so real as to demand the alerted attention and the active concern of all serious-minded persons. The author is at pains to delineate the exact nature and scope of the crisis and to present adequate, if not alarming, evidences of its stark reality. In order to give his readers a full view of the acute situation, he is careful to picture the background, sketch the different facets, and identify the specific factors involved. Then he points to the heart of the matter and proceeds to suggest a cure. Finally, he proposes a personal program for each one to follow, in company with others, for effecting a cure.

In dealing with a subject so ponderous and complicated as this, it is gratifying to note that the author has written with crystal clarity, in simple language easily comprehended by the average reader. This affords reason to believe that the most sophisticated cannot fail to understand its high meaning. It is also worthy of notice that he shows impressive mastery of the various phases of his subject.

To this writer, the key supplied by the author to the distressing conditions herein described is to be found in the reconcilement of our conflict in cultures. No one can behold the salient features of the crisis as here portrayed without recognizing this. The author believes that no civilization can exist apart from a religion. That religion must stand at the center and all things become oriented to it. In our Western world we have in the past essayed to make the Judeo-Christian concepts and their implied moral obligations the source of civilization. The failure now to gear all of life, individual and social, to this central force has caused the mischief. There are marginal contributory facts, to be sure, but they in no way change the chief cause of our plight. We should feel grateful that a discerning mind has furnished us with such a fair analysis of our predicament and has so faithfully revealed the way out.

As one in the nation's capital who is concerned with public affairs, who is permitted to observe the interplay of forces such as depicted in this arresting volume and thus is able to detect something of the trends, the stresses, and the accent seen in their interaction, I read this study avidly. I am amazed at the grasp, the comprehension, and penetration evident throughout. To attempt to give particulars would be to repeat poorly what is stated splendidly by the author.

Although the author is preoccupied with dark and sinister facts, he exhibits a robust faith. It is robust in the sense that, avoiding all Pollyanna optimism, he discovers much solid ground on which to base the social hope and preserves a sense of sure direction which will lead to a victorious goal of history. The book is therefore a strong tonic, curative and invigorating. As such, it constitutes a welcome contribution to the literature of remedial thought in our times. Armed with its vision, courage, and conviction, each of us should join the ranks of happy warriors in the victory march.

JOSEPH MARTIN DAWSON

Baptist Joint Committee on Public Affairs
Washington, D. C.

PREFACE

W HILE making a study in the field of Christianity and world issues, a chapter was developed on "Christianity and the World Crisis." The writing of that chapter brought a deepening conviction that the world situation is so acute that a separate volume on the crisis might be helpful.

My interest in the world crisis, however, has been of long standing. Several years ago, in co-operation with Dr. Frank K. Means, at that time professor of missions in the Southwestern Baptist Theological Seminary, and at the present time secretary for missionary education and promotion for the Foreign Mission Board of the Southern Baptist Convention, an experimental course was outlined and offered, in collaboration with other faculty members, on "Christianity and World Order." In recent years I have offered a similar course under the title "Christianity and the Crisis in Civilization." This book is the outgrowth of my continued interest and study in this field.

While the volume may be found acceptable for textbook purposes, it has been prepared primarily for general reading, for Christian ministers and laymen who are alert to the problems of the world and who are searching for a better understanding of the critical period in which we live.

An effort has been made to digest the best materials on the subject. While there are many excellent books on the world crisis, most of them emphasize only one particular phase of it. The present volume attempts to give some attention, although admittedly limited, to all the major phases of the crisis. On the other hand, the primary emphasis throughout is on the spiritual nature of the crisis, since it is believed that in every area of life it is basically spiritual.

I am conscious of the imperfections of the book. Some of these have resulted from the fact that the writing has been crowded into a busy teaching schedule, accompanied by frequent faculty and committee meetings, along with outside engagements typical of most college and seminary teachers. The careful reader will be conscious of considerable repetition in various chapters. Some of it was more or less unavoidable, since the various phases of the crisis are so closely interrelated. However, a certain amount of repetition has been done consciously and deliberately for emphasis. It represents a familiar teaching technique.

The following propositions set out briefly the major emphases and convictions that are woven into the total fabric of the book and provide the author's tentative conclusions.

1. *The world is in the midst of the most serious crisis it has known since the days of the Renaissance and the Reformation.*
2. *The present period of chaos, confusion, and travail is symptomatic of the existing crisis and will continue until the world gets beyond the crisis period.*
3. *This crisis is particularly acute in Western civilization.*

4. *The crisis in Western civilization is most acute in Western Europe, which has been the center of Western civilization and which has for various reasons experienced greater decay and collapse.*

5. *The crisis in the remainder of the world is related to and results from the crisis in Western civilization in some way and to some degree.*

6. *The contemporary crisis is so pervasive as to affect inevitably every phase of life.*

7. *A phenomenon of the proportions of the present crisis will have many contributing factors, both historical and contemporary. To attribute it to any one cause would be an oversimplification.*

8. *Although many factors have created the contemporary crisis, it is basically spiritual in its nature.*

9. *Since the cause of the crisis is basically spiritual, the remedy likewise must be primarily spiritual.*

10. *Simply stated, the contemporary crisis has resulted from the fact that man and his civilization have drifted away from God, and the only real remedy for it is for man and civilization to return to God and make him the integrating center of life.*

11. *This reintegration or reorientation of life must begin in the Christian church if the church is to be an effective instrument of God for the inner spiritual renewal of man and civilization.*

12. *Since God himself is the most determinative factor in the crisis, we should seek earnestly to discover the direction in which God is moving in our world.*

13. *The most important contribution we can make to the solution of the problems of the world is to pray for our world and for ourselves with an abiding faith that God is big enough to handle these problems and that his over-all purpose in the world ultimately will be accomplished.*

14. *With a strong faith in God we should seek to know and to do the will of God, knowing that nothing that we do for him will be lost.*

Grateful acknowledgments should be made to many. Various publishers gave permission to quote from many books, and the footnotes reveal some authors to whom I am heavily indebted. Others have contributed to my interpretation of the crisis, but their ideas have become so absorbed into my own thinking that I am unconscious of their source. I am particularly grateful to the students who have studied the world crisis with me. We have had many stimulating hours together. Some of them have read books at my direction, and in other ways they have helped me to locate and to evaluate materials.

I want to express my appreciation to Dr. L. R. Elliott, librarian of Southwestern Baptist Theological Seminary, who read most of the manuscript and who made many helpful suggestions for its improvement. I am also heavily indebted to Dr. J. M. Dawson, executive director of the Baptist Joint Committee on Public Affairs, and to the Honorable Brooks Hays, Representative of the Fifth District of

Arkansas in the United States Congress, both of whom
deal daily with important world affairs. They read the
manuscript, made valuable recommendations concerning
it, and have generously written the Foreword.

I am indebted to no one more than to Miss Marjorie
Stephens, who, in addition to a busy school program, pa-
tiently and efficiently typed and retyped the manuscript.

T. B. MASTON

1

EVIDENCES OF THE CRISIS

AFTER a 31,000-mile trip around the world made during World War II in 49 days, with only 161 hours of actual flying time, Wendell L. Willkie wrote a popular best seller entitled *One World*. He came back from the trip with the conviction that there were "no distant points in the world any longer," that the problems of the peoples of the Far East were as close to us as Los Angeles is to New York by the fastest train. He concluded, "Our thinking in the future must be world wide." [1]

In a world that has become one world, it is tragic for any citizen, particularly for any Christian citizen, to be narrow in his vision or limited in his sympathies. He should be big in mind and heart. He should think in world terms.

We have increasing evidence and a deepening conviction in recent years that the world is in a major crisis. Some of the keenest students of world affairs consider this crisis the

[1] Wendell L. Willkie, *One World* (New York: Simon and Schuster, 1943), p. 2.

I

most serious that the world has known since the days of the Renaissance and the Reformation. They contend that a whole new way of life is in the process of being born, that the present period of travail will continue until the new world is born, and that this new order will affect deeply our nation and every other nation of the world. Although the crisis is most acute within Western civilization, yet all peoples of the world, even those in the remotest areas, will be affected by it.

It is difficult for people who are in the midst of a crisis to understand its nature, to analyze properly the factors creating it, to understand the direction in which it is moving, or even to be conscious of its existence. We are all better historians than we are prophets.

Most of the succeeding chapters, in one way or another, provide some evidence of the contemporary world crisis. We shall consider in the present chapter a few general evidences of the crisis.

CONDITIONS WITHIN OUR NATION

The logical place to begin a search for evidences of the present crisis is within our own nation. Considerable evidence indicates that our nation is in the midst of the most serious crisis period it has known since the War Between the States. What happens within our nation in the next few years doubtless will determine the direction in which it will move for the indefinite future and the place it will fill in world affairs.

We might properly discuss many angles of the national crisis. At least one evidence that is of major importance is the changing attitude of the people toward their government, particularly the Federal Government. It is basic in the democratic philosophy of government that the state exists for the sake of the individual.

In the early days of the democratic movement, which gave birth to our nation, it was thought that the chief functions of the state in relation to its citizens were to provide freedom and justice for all the people. In recent days, as a more or less natural result of our materialistic way of life, our nation and other nations have tended to place more emphasis on the provision of economic security for their citizens—with "security" being interpreted very liberally. It is no mere accident that one of the famous "Four Freedoms" of Franklin Delano Roosevelt and Winston Churchill was freedom from want. Its inclusion was symptomatic of the age.

Too many of our people have come to depend upon their government for economic security, which has tended to make them indifferent regarding their own responsibilities as citizens. This attitude seems to be growing more prevalent and is a real threat to our democratic way of life. This is not said, however, to disparage in any way the essential welfare services of our government.

Some consider the threat of communism as the chief source of our national crisis. Without minimizing the challenge of communism, it should be said that communism is, and will be, a threat to the degree that our nation has become decadent and weak within. The chief threat to our nation is not from without but from within.

The heart of the crisis in the United States is not economic or political but moral and spiritual. The chief trouble, even within the economic and political areas, stems from the moral and spiritual conditions which threaten the very foundation of our nation. Our government was founded upon deep moral convictions and high spiritual principles, and our democratic way of life cannot be maintained indefinitely apart from these high concepts and ideals.

Our forefathers laid well the foundations of our nation. They were the first to crystallize into political institutions the democratic ideas that grew out of the Protestant Reformation and the revival of humanism during the Renaissance.

In the cluster of democratic concepts that provided much of the foundation for the establishment of our nation, none was more basic than the idea of the dignity and worth of the individual. This respect for human personality was, and is, largely a heritage from the Christian religion, not only to our nation but to Western civilization. The Christian view is that the individual is of more value than all things material. This high value placed on man is related to and dependent upon the fact that man is made in the image of God. It is his actual or potential relation to God that gives him his dignity and worth.

Who would dare say that we have not departed a long way, at least in practice, from this fundamental position? The materialization and secularization of life have gone so far that tools, machines, and material things are generally considered of more value than man. Such an evaluation, if continued, will destroy the foundations of our traditional American way of life. The materialistic concept may provide the basis for a socialistic, a communistic, or a fascistic regime, but not for a democracy.

The existing materialism and paganism may be a more or less natural expression of the humanistic source of democracy. Humanism has tended to divorce itself from God and to give man supreme value apart from God. Instead of this view exalting man, it really debases him and pulls him down to the level of the natural and the material. When he is measured in material terms, man becomes of secondary value.

The American way of life also has been built upon the moral integrity of the average citizen and of those in places of leadership. The continuance of the democratic way of life is dependent upon such moral integrity, as well as upon a high degree of general and political intelligence.

The Congressional investigations, the newspapers, and the magazines have revealed in recent years appalling weaknesses in the moral fiber of our American people, including political leadership at the top level. They have revealed that there has been, and is, a definite connection between organized crime and organized politics in many, and possibly in all, of our larger American cities. We have many other evidences of corruption in high places—conduct that at least revealed a lack of moral sensitivity.

Then we find in the home and individual life much evidence of the inner decay of our nation. The divorce rate is the highest of any Western nation. In one recent year there were thirty-one divorces for every hundred marriages, with some large cities having more applications for divorce decrees than for marriage licenses. Note also the loosening of sex morality. The Kinsey report,[2] even if it is only relatively correct, paints a dark picture of the sexual practices and attitudes of the human male. The history of nations and civilizations reveals that there is no surer sign of the approaching destruction of a nation or the collapse of a civilization than the breakdown of sex morals and the decay of the home.

We should remind ourselves that an abundance of natu-

[2] Alfred C. Kinsey, *Sexual Behavior in the Human Male* (Philadelphia: W. B. Saunders Co., 1948).

ral resources, economic prosperity, and military might will not and cannot save our nation if we become morally decadent. History would teach us that the decline and fall of the great nations of the world came about because moral decay had eaten away their strength and vitality. They did not have the stamina to withstand the challenges from within and from without. Their overthrow was inevitable.

At least one thing in the whole picture should give us some encouragement: Enough health is left in our body politic to make possible the Congressional investigations of recent years. We have seen also that at least some of our people can be aroused concerning the conditions in our society.

THE GENERAL WORLD SITUATION

The evidences of the present crisis are found not only within our nation but also within other nations and in the world in general. It is not only national but also international in its scope. The entire world has been in one continuous and, in some ways, ever-deepening struggle from the opening days of World War I. The war itself came as a rather rude shock to the unrealistic idealists who thought the world was about to enter the golden age of peace and good will among men. The political and religious liberals thought that all that was necessary for man to solve his problems and the problems of his world was to give him more knowledge, more power, and more freedom.

Much of this idealism was carried into the prosecution of World War I and provided some of the drive and motivation for many Americans who participated in it. They thought of it as a war to make the world safe for democracy, a war to end all wars. What a tragic disillusionment there was for many of the peoples of our nation and of the other nations of the world!

Some prophetic souls realized early that World War I was not an isolated event. For example, Albert Schweitzer, writing between World Wars I and II, said, "The war, with everything connected with it, is only a phenomenon of the condition of our un-civilization in which we find ourselves." [3] World War I was the first major outward manifestation of the world crisis, which has continued until today and may continue for many years.

We cannot trace all the varying expressions of the mounting crisis through the intervening years. The League of Nations, with all the high hopes for it in spite of its evident weaknesses from the beginning and its failure when faced with a real emergency in the world, was both an element in the crisis and an evidence of how deeply the crisis had penetrated the social fabric of the world.

The depression periods, particularly the great depression beginning in the fall of 1929, were factors in the crisis but also evidences of it. Really, many of the nations of the world did not make any appreciable recovery from the great depression until they began to rearm for World War II. This itself reveals the seriousness of the crisis.

World War II was a war very few people wanted to fight, and yet millions were unmercifully forced into it. It was more widespread and more devastating than any the world had ever known. It lacked the high idealism characteristic of World War I. For the West, it was at best a defensive war.

Although Italy, Germany, and Japan were defeated, one wonders if World War II has really ended or if we are al-

[3] Albert Schweitzer, *Civilization and Ethics* (London: A. & C. Black, Ltd., 2nd ed., 1929), p. 1.

ready in the preliminary stages of World War III; and if so, it will undoubtedly be more destructive by far than World War II. Fantastic weapons for destruction and defense are being perfected. Some students of world affairs believe that another global conflict would mean the destruction of what we call civilization.

The preceding is not a beautiful picture, but one cannot be realistic and paint a rosy picture of the world in which we live. This somber picture is strong evidence of the seriousness of the modern crisis. A study of the history of civilizations will reveal that any period of major transition has been characterized by chaos, confusion, and conflict. The present travail in our world is an evidence that the world is in a major transition period, that we have not yet found a solution for the current crisis, and that the new way of life that is struggling to be born has not come to birth.

THE CONTEMPORARY FRAME OF MIND

The contemporary frame of mind, created to a considerable degree by the modern world situation, is another evidence of the seriousness of the world crisis. Incidentally, it should be said that this frame of mind is due not only to the conditions which people face, but also in a large degree, to their lack of moral strength and inner spiritual resources to face squarely, courageously, and successfully those conditions. Instead of letting the conditions in the world challenge them, they surrender fatalistically to them.

This does not mean that the individual should resist all the changes that are a part of the present transition. He should accept some of them. Certainly, when he once senses the direction in which the world should move (not necessarily is moving), he should co-operate enthusiastically, although intelligently, with such movement. Only weaklings will refuse to make some effort to help.

The do-nothing sense of futility which is so prevalent, particularly among young people, and even among intelligent young people, is a contributor to, and an evidence of, the crisis. So many say: "There isn't anything that I can do. The forces that move the world toward a deepening crisis are impersonal and irresistible. There is nothing that an individual can do about it."

There are some, of course, who are not alert enough to sense that there is a crisis in the world. Some, in spite of the foreboding clouds around them, are incurable optimists. They are the ones who, to use a phrase of Lewis Mumford's, do not include "a Dark Age in their chronology" and who, "like the sun dial, . . . cannot tell time on a stormy day." [4] Such unrealistic optimists are not restricted to any class or age group.

Then a spirit of frustration and confusion frequently characterizes even those who are concerned about the world situation. They sense that the world is sitting on a powder keg with a burning fuse attached. They feel the urgency of the situation. They are not willing to resign themselves to the inevitable. They want to do something, but their question is, What can we do? This is not the same as a sense of futility, although it may be closely related to it. Those who are thus frustrated and confused feel that they are not making an effective contribution. They want additional light which will help them to function more effectively in this critical era.

Such futility, frustration, and confusion on the part of many people reflect more or less accurately the conditions

[4] Lewis Mumford, *Faith for Living* (New York: Harcourt, Brace & Co., 1940), p. 121.

in the world. Many people throughout the world have a feeling that their leaders are about as confused as they are. Judged by the directions in which most nations have moved in military strategy and foreign policy, one properly could conclude that the leaders of those nations do not know where they are going or the direction in which the world is moving.

Another evidence of the chaotic conditions in our world is the increasing prevalence of nervous and mental disorders. The whole attitude in regard to mental disease has been too much hush-hush. The taboo, however, is being removed gradually and a more wholesome approach is being made to the treatment and care of the mentally ill. But we do not realize, even yet, the proportions of mental illness in the United States. Few know that there are more than 125,000 Americans admitted to mental hospitals each year; that on an average day in a recent year there were 635,769 patients in institutions for mental and nervous diseases in the United States, and that the mental patients represent a little more than half the total number of hospital patients in the United States in a single day. It is also estimated that for every patient now in a mental hospital there is another on the outside who should have special care and treatment in a psychiatric institution; that 8,000,000 Americans are suffering from some kind of mental illness. Of the 4,800,-000 draft registrants rejected as unfit for military service during World War II, 1,700,000 were turned down for mental or neurological diseases or defects.[5] It is assumed that conditions in the United States are no worse than they are in many other nations.

D. Elton Trueblood suggests that we can discover what

[5] Albert Deutsch, *The Shame of the States* (New York: Harcourt, Brace & Co., 1948), pp. 30-1.

people do not have by what they frantically seek. The disturbed condition of men's minds is revealed by the growing popularity and the phenomenal sale of such publications as Rabbi Liebman's *Peace of Mind* and Norman Vincent Peale's *A Guide to Confident Living*.

Trueblood also suggests that the modern frame of mind is revealed by what draws the crowds. Albert Schweitzer, during a recent visit to the United States, could not equal in drawing power a high school basketball tournament. Judging by the experience at the University of California, the only speaker who could draw a crowd as large as a university basketball game was Professor Kinsey, of the University of Indiana, who, along with others, is the author of *Sexual Behavior in the Human Male*. Trueblood suggests that it was the subject of the professor and not his eloquence that drew the crowd, and then rather disturbingly concludes: "The subject would have been equally successful in drawing crowds in ancient Rome, especially in its period of decay." [6]

This chaotic, confused, frustrated frame of mind is revealed in every phase of modern man's life. Sorokin suggests that "the fine arts are one of the sensitive mirrors of the society and culture of which they are an important part. What the society and culture are, such will their fine arts be." [7] If that is true, then one look at most modern art will reveal a very confused state of mind.

The fact that some evangelists are preaching to overflow audiences seems, on the surface, to contradict the preceding. A closer examination will reveal, however, that the large audiences at such meetings may be explained, to some

[6] D. Elton Trueblood, *Signs of Hope in a Century of Despair* (New York: Harper & Bros., 1950), p. 22.

[7] Pitirim A. Sorokin, *The Crisis of Our Age* (New York: E. P. Dutton & Co., Inc., 1941), p. 30.

degree, by the fact that people generally are frustrated and confused, are searching for certainty, and are frantically seeking for something that will give them purpose and power for life and its complex problems.

MODERN WORLD MOVEMENTS

Another evidence that the world is in the midst of a crisis of major proportions is the rise and growth of economic, political, and religious movements that compete with one another and also challenge the generally accepted ways of life. These movements are both creations of and are creators of the crisis. This is true whether we are thinking of socialism, communism, fascism, totalitarianism in general, existentialism in the field of philosophy, Neo-Protestantism in theological circles, or the resurgence of Roman Catholicism in many areas of the world.

Most of these movements have their roots deep in the past. For example, the Communist Manifesto was written by Marx and Engels over a hundred years ago (1848). This and their other writings, particularly those of Marx, have been the inspiration for the socialist and communist movements of the past century. Marxism, as interpreted by Lenin and as reinterpreted and applied by Stalin, is the chief challenger of what has been accepted for several centuries as the way of life for Western civilization.

The preceding paragraph sounds as if Marxism, with the movements that have stemmed from it, had created the present crisis. We must admit that it has been a factor in the crisis; but Marxism, as expressed through modern socialist movements, and particularly as interpreted and applied by the so-called Communists of today, has had its great opportunity for growth because the world is in a crisis.

An effective phase of the strategy of the Communists is to create and to deepen in every way possible the sense of frustration and fear, of chaos and confusion. They want the peoples of the nations of the world to arrive at such a state of hopelessness that they will accept the promises of communism and turn to it as their savior. The prevalence of such a frame of mind explains the comparative ease with which the Communists have taken over some of the nations of the world. This simply means that the contemporary rise of communism is a symptom of the diseased status of the world.

Likewise, fascistic totalitarian regimes have arisen in our day because of the conditions of the world. Their rise, spread, and tremendous influence are due to the fact that the world is in a crisis. They arose because the people were searching for some means that would give them peace and order, that would provide for them the sense of security for which they deeply longed. Unfortunately, many men had gotten their values so badly confused that they were willing to surrender the freedoms for which men in times past had died that they might gain a sense of economic security and well-being. This helps to explain the rise to power of such men as Mussolini, Hitler, Franco, and Peron.

It should be stated, of course, that communism as it has developed in the Soviet Union is totalitarian. It claims that it is a dictatorship of the proletariat rather than an individual dictatorship. But it is a dictatorship. Originally the Communists proposed that the proletariat dictatorship would be temporary; that it would be a necessary phase of the transition from a capitalistic, class-conscious society to a classless way of life. Once the latter was attained, it was suggested that there would be no longer a need for the dictatorship. It seems, however, that the dictatorial powers at the present are being tightened instead of relaxed. There are some evidences that even the theory concerning the temporary nature of the dictatorship and the "withering state" is in the process of being revised.[8] Whether the dictatorship is fascistic or communistic, it has arisen because our world is in the midst of a crisis.

One phase of the modern crisis is that concerning man and within man. The traditional viewpoint in the West has been, and is, that man is of supreme value. This basic concept has a twofold source—humanism and the Christian religion. There was no serious conflict between these two sources so long as humanism was primarily theocentric. The high value that Christianity places on man stems from the fact that man was made in the image of God; that he was made for fellowship with God. It may sound paradoxical, but so long as man recognizes his relation to, and his dependence upon, God, such an attitude contributes to his exaltation. The ultimate result in man's life of his divorcement from God, which is a natural result of a nontheistic humanism, was, and is, a loss of a sense of personal worth and dignity. He also tends to lose his faith in himself.

When man loses his faith in God and in himself, he tends to turn to someone or something that will help him to recapture his sense of dignity and importance. Millions have done this in our day by turning to a strong, centralized party or state. In other words, the modern movements that challenge the ways of the West have become strong in our day because of the inner conflicts and weaknesses of man, which weaknesses in turn are indicative of the inner weaknesses of our civilization.

Another evidence of the world crisis, which will be dis-

[8] Andrei Y. Vyshinsky (editor), *The Law of the Soviet State* (New York: The Macmillan Co., 1948), pp. 60–62.

cussed more fully later, is the trend toward a worldwide political organization of some type and a companion trend or movement toward a world ecclesiastical organization. Here we are not seeking to evaluate these movements but merely to suggest that the interest in such movements and the trends in that direction are additional symptoms or evidences of the critical situation in our world.

It is hard to determine how much the trend toward political and ecclesiastical universalism represents the shape of the future and how much it is simply an evidence of the sense of futility and frustration of the contemporary period. There is at least a possibility that the ecumenical movement may be an evidence of the decadent condition of the heart of civilization. This movement, as well as the one toward political universalism, may represent man's attempt to revitalize and to strengthen his way of life by an external reorientation of life rather than by an inner renewal of life. There may be in the movements an evidence of man's blind hope that by revamping the machinery he can recapture the moral and spiritual power that has so largely been lost.

Other movements, more philosophical and theological, are also evidences of the critical nature of the contemporary period. Nicholas Berdyaev, Russian-born philosopher and one of the keenest students of world movements, says that the Western leaders of thought with the most influence in the contemporary period are Marx, Nietzsche, and Kierkegaard.[9]

Marx doubtless has more devotees than any other man living or dead with the exception of Jesus of Nazareth. Nietzsche's influence has not been so extensive, direct, or personal as that of Marx. His writings or theories do not ap-

[9] Nicholas Berdyaev, *Towards a New Epoch* (London: Geoffrey Bles, 1949), p. 111.

peal strongly to the masses of men. His belittling of Christian love and sympathy, the central place he gives to the will-to-power, and his idea of the superman are definitely inimical to the best interests of the masses. Usually those who have followed Nietzsche's theories, which is the way of totalitarian dictatorship, have had to fool the people to gain control over them.

On the other hand, it might be said correctly that modern communism promises one thing and produces another. It has promised to the underprivileged liberty and freedom, but wherever it has gained power it has enslaved. Theoretically, the philosophies of Marx and Nietzsche do not have much in common. However, as Marxism has been worked out in practice by the Communists, the ultimate results of the way of Marx and Nietzsche are largely the same.

The third member of the group to which Berdyaev has ascribed so much influence is Kierkegaard, the philosopher. He was comparatively unknown until the world entered into the present crisis period. It was discovered that his philosophy, with its emphasis on living for the moment, is well adapted to the contemporary frame of mind—particularly the frame of mind of many European peoples whose civilization has become so decadent.

It is no mere accident that the most distinctive theological movement of the contemporary period is Neo-Protestantism. The whole temper and spirit of the movement belong within the framework of a crisis period. The early leaders of the movement were indebted considerably to the philosophical school of Kierkegaard.

There were many factors that led to the rise of Neo-Protestantism. It represents among other things a more or less natural reaction to the social gospel movement, or possibly more accurately to the liberal theology which had so largely captured the social gospel movement and which was primarily man-centered rather than God-centered. This liberal theology became little more than a theistic humanism. It professed a strong but unrealistic faith in man's ability to solve his own problems and the problems of his world. According to this school of thought, all man needed in order to solve his problems and the problems of his society were more knowledge, which education could and would give him; more power, which science was in the process of giving to him; and more freedom, which the democratic movement could and would give him. The tragedies of recent years—World War I, the great depression, World War II, and the mounting crisis in the world—exploded this blind, unrealistic dream or hope. Men everywhere, including many of the liberals, became terribly disillusioned. It was increasingly recognized in most circles that sin was a more serious matter, both in the life of the individual and in society, than most liberal theologians had suggested.

From such a background the new theology arose. More or less naturally it arose first in Europe, where the crisis has progressed further than elsewhere. The spread of the movement and the wide acceptance and influence of Neo-Protestantism, or Neo-supernaturalism, cannot be explained apart from the sense of crisis that is gripping so many of the peoples of the world. While most of its leading exponents have come out of the liberal tradition, its influence is felt in all theological circles. This is true in America as well as in Europe.

It is rather interesting, and also natural, that the Neo-Protestant movement in America should differ in some ways from the movement in Europe. Reinhold Niebuhr, who belongs within the Neo-Protestant tradition and who generally is considered one of the great, if not the greatest,

American theologian, goes much further than Barth or even Brunner—the leading European Neo-Protestants—in his ethical emphasis and in giving man a place in the work of God. In Niebuhr, there is really a fusion, to a considerable degree, of Neo-Protestantism, a creation of Europe, with the social gospel emphasis, which is a product of American Christianity.

One other word should be said about these modern economic, political, and religious movements. Although they are evidences of the contemporary crisis, they do not necessarily point the direction in which the world is going to move. Their rise may be merely symptomatic of the diseased condition of the world. On the other hand, if there are common elements in a number of these movements, this fact might give some hint of the direction in which the world may move. At least it is possible that these and other movements, arising at the time when the old ways are being challenged and changed, may determine, to some degree, the shape of things to come. They are, at least for the present, on the offensive, while the old ways are on the defensive. It remains to be seen whether the old ways can adjust themselves to the changing conditions and can discover the springs of renewal to the degree that they can recapture the initiative in the struggle for the soul of the world. Time alone will reveal the full details of the shape of the future.

THE VERDICT OF THE SCHOLARS

Students of world affairs agree almost universally that the modern world is in the midst of a major crisis. This is the verdict of statesmen, historians, social scientists, philosophers, and religious leaders. Some may and do believe that the present crisis means the death of contemporary civilization, while others think of it as the birth pangs of a new civilization. Practically all of them agree, however, that the world has not known any crisis comparable to it in seriousness since the days of the Renaissance and the Reformation. The latter was the general period which gave birth to what is known as modern civilization.

One of those who sensed the approaching crisis early, and one who really was a prophet of doom, was Oswald Spengler. He conceived his general approach before World War I and had the manuscript fully worked out by 1917. The book appeared in Germany in 1918, and was later translated into English.[10] The two big volumes (brought out in a one-volume edition in 1932) represented an attempt at a philosophy of history that, from the author's viewpoint, would explain the decay, the decline, and what he conceived to be the approaching death of Western civilization. Spengler's viewpoint was that civilizations go through a life cycle just as do individuals. A civilization is born, which is followed by a childhood and a youth period, a period of full maturity, and then old age, senility, and ultimately death. It was his conviction that the processes of death for Western civilization had already set in.

Other students of world affairs early shared Spengler's insight into the approaching crisis but not necessarily his pessimism concerning the ultimate outcome. For example, the opening sentence of Chapter 1 of Albert Schweitzer's *Civilization and Ethics,* copyrighted in 1923, is: "Our civilization is going through a severe crisis." [11] He suggested there, as he did elsewhere, that the crisis was not produced by World War I, but that the war was an evidence or a

[10] Oswald Spengler, *The Decline of the West* (New York: Alfred A. Knopf, Inc., 1926, 1928.)
[11] *Op. cit.,* p. 1.

manifestation of the crisis [12] which dated back to the middle of the nineteenth century.[13]

As early as 1919, Nicholas Berdyaev said: "Contemporary history is being wound up. An unknown era is upon us." [14] Some years later, the same author said: "It has become a banality to say that we live in a time of historical crisis, that a whole epoch is ending, and a new one, as yet without a name, is beginning." [15] Again, several years later, we find Berdyaev still emphasizing the same theme: "A whole epoch of history is coming to an end, . . . an entire civilization is on the point of perishing, and . . . we are on the eve of witnessing the emergence of a new world the outlines of which are still not clearly defined." [16] Although a Russian, Berdyaev was not a Communist.

Many other European scholars of more recent years have similarly emphasized the critical nature of the days in which we live. We see this emphasis in the writings of such men as the German-born English professor of economics, Karl Mannheim,[17] the somewhat left-wing scholar for and leader in the British Labor Party, Harold J. Laski,[18] and the

[12] Albert Schweitzer, *The Decay and Restoration of Civilization* (London: A. & C. Black, Ltd., 1923), p. 1.

[13] *Ibid.*, p. 9.

[14] Nicholas Berdyaev, *The End of Our Time* (New York: Sheed and Ward, 1933), p. 11. See note, p. 8, for dating of above statement.

[15] Nicholas Berdyaev, *The Fate of Man in the Modern World* (New York-Milwaukee: Morehouse Publishing Co., 1935), p. 1.

[16] Nicholas Berdyaev, *Towards a New Epoch* (London: Geoffrey Bles, 1949), p. v.

[17] Karl Mannheim, *Man and Society in an Age of Reconstruction* (New York: Harcourt, Brace & Co., 1941), *Diagnosis of Our Time* (New York: Oxford University Press, 1944), and *Freedom, Power, and Democracy* (New York: Oxford University Press, 1950).

[18] Harold J. Laski, *Reflections on the Revolution of Our Times* (New York: The Viking Press, 1943), *Faith, Reason, and Civilization* (New York: The Viking Press, 1944), and *The Dilemma in Our Times* (London: George Allen and Unwin Ltd., 1952).

French-Catholic philosopher, Jacques Maritain.[19] To Maritain, the present period is one of general liquidation for the world. He suggests that the end of the Roman Empire was a minor event compared to what we face today.[20]

Other European writers have continued more recently to hammer home the same general thesis. For example, D. R. Davies suggests that there is only one prospect for Western civilization, and that is "rapidly accumulating contradictions and conflicts and accelerating disintegration," [21] while H. D. A. Major says, " 'The breakdown of civilization' is the name we give to a collapse of those moral and spiritual foundations on which our western civilization has been built." [22] Although Arnold Toynbee rather optimistically suggests that mankind "is always and everywhere in danger of exaggerating the historical importance of contemporary events," [23] yet the popularity of his approach to history results, to a large degree, from a sense of impending crisis.

While it is natural that the sense of crisis would not be so acute in the United States as it is in Europe where the actual disintegration has progressed much further, yet there is an increasing awareness of the crisis by American students of world affairs. The Russian-born sociologist, Pitirim A. Sorokin, has possibly given more attention to the world crisis than any other American scholar.[24] D. Elton

[19] See particularly his *The Twilight of Civilization* (New York: Sheed and Ward, 1943).

[20] Jacques Maritain, *Christianity and Democracy* (New York: Charles Scribner's Sons, 1944), p. 17.

[21] D. R. Davies, *The Sin of Our Age* (New York: The Macmillan Co., 1947), p. 123.

[22] H. D. A. Major, *Civilization and Religious Values* (London: George Allen & Unwin, Ltd., 1948), p. 25.

[23] Arnold Toynbee, *Civilization on Trial* (New York: Oxford University Press, 1948), p. 63.

[24] See particularly *The Crisis of Our Age* (New York: E. P. Dutton & Co., Inc., 1941).

Trueblood, with his brief, concise analyses, has captured the attention of an uneasy American public. His *The Predicament of Modern Man* [25] is a clear, concise statement of the general world situation. Other books by the same author and with the same general theme, all of which are rather brief, are: *Foundations for Reconstruction* (1946); *Alternative to Futility* (1948); *Signs of Hope* (1950); and *The Life We Prize* (1951).

Other Americans with varying backgrounds and positions have recognized the seriousness of the contemporary crisis. This is true of philosophers such as Ralph T. Flewelling [26] and Lewis Mumford; [27] a sociologist such as Charles A. Ellwood; [28] economists such as J. B. Condliffe [29] and Eugene Staley; [30] statesmen and politicians such as Herbert Hoover and Hugh Gibson; [31] and columnists such as Walter Lippman and Dorothy Thompson.

Although lacking the depth of understanding of the scholars in other fields, with few exceptions, the writers of religious books show some insight into the seriousness of the contemporary crisis. The consciousness of the crisis is evident in recent publications by such popular religious leaders and writers as Harry Emerson Fosdick and Leslie D. Weatherhead. This awareness is particularly acute in the

[25] D. Elton Trueblood, *The Predicament of Modern Man* (New York: Harper & Bros., 1944).

[26] Ralph T. Flewelling, *The Survival of Western Culture* (New York: Harper & Bros., 1943).

[27] Lewis Mumford, *Faith for Living* (New York: Harcourt, Brace & Co., 1940).

[28] Charles A. Ellwood, *The World's Need of Christ* (New York-Nashville: Abingdon-Cokesbury Press, 1940).

[29] J. B. Condliffe, *The Reconstruction of World Trade: a Survey of International Economic Relations* (New York: W. W. Norton & Co., 1940).

[30] Eugene Staley, *World Economy in Transition* (New York: Council on Foreign Relations, 1939).

[31] Herbert Hoover and Hugh Gibson, *The Problems of Lasting Peace* (New York: Doubleday, Doran and Co., Inc., 1942).

writings of E. Stanley Jones, who has been predicting for many years a crisis in the West. Possibly no American theologian has a deeper sense of the crisis than Reinhold Niebuhr. As long ago as 1934, he wrote a book entitled *Reflections on the End of an Era.*[32] Although he was referring primarily to the end of an economic era, the book is quite predictive. He has been editing now for a number of years a publication entitled *Christianity and Crisis.* His strong sense of crisis may be one reason for his popularity in Europe, particularly in Great Britain. Walter Horton's *Can Christianity Save Civilization?* [33] is a book of major importance on the present crisis.

There are many other writers who reveal, to a more or less degree, an awareness of the crisis; these are cited merely as proof that many world scholars in various fields of learning are conscious of the seriousness of the contemporary crisis. Such an awareness by students of world affairs is one evidence of the actual existence of the crisis.

[32] New York: Charles Scribner's Sons, 1934.
[33] New York: Harper & Bros., 1940.

2

BACKGROUND OF THE CRISIS

A NY major crisis in the life of an individual, a nation,
or a civilization has its roots in the past. This is
particularly true of a crisis of the proportions of
the present one. An understanding of its background will
give a clearer insight into its causes, timing, nature, direction, and possible solutions.

In tracing the background of the crisis, we shall limit ourselves to Western civilization. The contemporary crisis is
worldwide in scope, but the crises in other areas of the
world are closely related to the crisis in the West.

Western civilization has become the dominant civilization in the world and has been exported to other parts of
the world. A civilization as complex, as aggressive, and as
missionary as Western civilization could not export merely
its technical skills. Some of its ideas and ideals inevitably
went along with its machines and techniques. These became competitors with the ideas and ideals of other cultures and civilizations. As the new ideas and ideals began

24

to germinate, the result was tension and conflict at the heart of those cultures.

Of all the ideas exported by the West to the far corners of the earth, there was none more important and significant than the high value that it placed upon the individual. Respect for human personality as such, which is as distinctive as any basic ideal of Western civilization, was largely though not exclusively a contribution of Christianity. Whenever any Christian principle takes root among a people, there begins a reorientation of life around that principle. The period of reorientation or transition will always be a time of strife and struggle, of chaos and confusion.

In addition to restricting ourselves to Western civilization, we shall limit this background study to the Christian era. This is considered sufficient for our purposes, although it is recognized that the fullest understanding of the background would require a broader coverage. Brief consideration will be given to the Grecian and Roman elements in Western civilization, but there will be no attempt to trace those influences beyond the Christian era. One reason for this limitation is the fact that the contemporary crisis is primarily spiritual in its nature.

SOURCES OF WESTERN CIVILIZATION

While there are many sources, direct and indirect, of Western civilization, we shall consider only the three major ones here: the Grecian, the Hebrew-Christian, and the Roman.[1] John Macmurray says that these three influences or

[1] Herbert von Beckerath, *In Defense of the West: a political and economic study* (Durham, N. C.: Duke University, 1942), p. 31 credits contributions from Celtic, Germanic, and Slavic tribes.

old civilizations have been mixed together to form our culture and that the three never have been fully fused. He suggests that the Hebrew element represents religion, the Grecian element art, and the Roman element organization and administration. The latter has made, or at least attempted to make, the Grecian and Hebrew elements of art and religion subservient to the Roman. According to Macmurray, the crises in the development of Europe have arisen when the Greek and Christian elements rebelled against the dominance and control of the Roman. The period of the Renaissance (representing in the main the Greek element) and the Reformation (representing primarily the Hebrew-Christian element) was such a period of rebellion.[2]

We find much truth in Macmurray's general viewpoint, although there are some limitations to it. There is general agreement concerning the three main sources of Western civilization. It is a mistake, however, to suggest, if Macmurray intended to do so, that the sole, or even the chief, contribution of Greece to Western civilization was its art. If we consider the Greek contribution to the ideas and ideals of the West—and these are the fabric out of which a civilization is woven—then we must recognize that Greece's main contribution to the West was through her philosophy and philosophers.

For study purposes, it may be justifiable to consider separately the Grecian, Hebrew-Christian, and Roman elements of our civilization; yet we should remember that, in reality, no clear distinctions can be made. It is true, as Macmurray says, that they have never been fully fused, but they do possess some common elements and have been influenced by one another.

[2] See John Macmurray, *Freedom in the Modern World* (London: Faber & Faber, 1948), pp. 74–83.

For example, the high value placed on the individual, which is such a distinctive element in Western civilization, is usually considered a contribution by Christianity to the West. While this is largely true, it is not all the truth. This concept, although on a somewhat different basis, is found in some Greek philosophy. It is humanistic as well as Christian. It is possible that the humanism of the Renaissance period was indebted, to a considerable degree, to the Christian movement for its concept of the individual's worth. It is even possible that the Greek and Roman elements in Western civilization are indebted to the Hebrew-Christian element for some of their influence in Western civilization. They were adopted and adapted by the Christian movement and, to a degree, became an integral part of the movement. Walter Horton suggests that the Greek spirit contributed to Western culture as it was assimilated by Christianity.[3]

Regardless of how much or how little tension these three elements of Western civilization have created at the heart of our civilization, they are the chief elements in it. The contemporary crisis cannot be understood apart from some comprehension of these three sources which, to a degree, have been fused and yet continue to be competing elements in our way of life.

THE EARLY CHRISTIAN CENTURIES

Although faced with an unfriendly world and at times a persecuting state, the Christian movement spread very rap-

---

[3] Walter Horton, *Can Christianity Save Civilization?* p. 67. See T. C. Hall's *History of Ethics Within Organized Christianity* (London: T. Fisher Unwin, 1910), chapter 3, for a discussion of the conflict of these three elements within the church.

idly during the first three or four hundred years of the Christian era. Latourette says: "Never in so short a time has any religious faith, or, for that matter, any other set of ideas, religious, political, or economic, without the aid of physical force or of social or cultural prestige, achieved so commanding a position in such an important culture." [4] The political power, which had sought to eliminate the Christian movement, capitulated and attempted to make an ally of its former foe. The Christian movement became not only the dominant religious influence but also the dominant power in the Roman Empire. It became an integral part of the civilization of the medieval world. The barbarians of northern Europe overran the medieval world, but they stood in awe of that world, recognizing that it contained a higher culture than their own. The fact that Christianity was a part of that culture was one reason for the friendly attitude of the peoples of the north toward the Christian movement. "It was through these same peoples of the northern shores of the Mediterranean and of Northern Europe that Christianity achieved the geographical advances of the sixteenth, seventeenth, eighteenth, and nineteenth centuries which have made it the most widely professed faith of mankind." [5]

This is not all the picture. The church, which during the first two or three centuries challenged and largely separated itself from the world, gradually made its peace with the world. While it became an integral part of the culture or the environment surrounding it, that culture or environment in turn tended to become an integral part of the Christian movement. This process of mutual infiltration

[4] Kenneth Scott Latourette, *A History of the Expansion of Christianity*, Vol. I, "The First Five Centuries" (New York: Harper & Bros., 1937), p. 112.
[5] *Ibid.*, p. 113.

and identification was not universal, but it was characteristic of the main stream of the Christian movement. The church's ceremonies and forms of worship and even her doctrines became a strange mixture of Christian and pagan elements.

Several factors contributed to the compromise of the church with the world. In general, the Christian movement tended to lose much of the vitality and the virility of the earlier period. It is possible that the decrease, and ultimately the cessation, of persecution was at least a negative factor in that change. Another contributing factor was the spread of Christianity among the official and upper classes. The temptations were greater for them to make some adjustments to the world and to the things of the world than was true of the poorer people, who composed most of the early adherents to the Christian religion.

It is also true that middle and upper-class people usually have many interests in addition to their church. Often they are prone to restrict their religion to one phase of life and not to let it influence too much the other areas of life. Religion for them is not ordinarily the dominant interest, the integrating center of their lives. It tends to become a mere appendage or a convenience to life.

At a comparatively early period also was felt the influence of second and third generation Christians who lacked the warmth and depth of conviction of their fathers who were converted from paganism, or at least from Judaism. This does not mean that second and third generation Christians necessarily will be lacking in vitality and virility, but it does mean that there is a very real danger at this point.

Another matter contributing to the loss of the original vitality of the Christian movement was the decreasing hope

of the early return of the Lord. This loss of hope was a factor in the reorientation of the church in its relation to the
world. If the Lord was to return soon, then Christians
might wisely withdraw as far as possible from the affairs
of the world. On the other hand, if they believed that the
Lord's return might be delayed indefinitely, then likely they
would conclude that it would be wise for them to work out
a long-term strategy concerning the church's relation to the
world and the program to overcome the world. This long-
term strategy frequently has included a considerable adjustment to the world, an adjustment that has bordered upon,
if it has not actually involved, compromise. A sense of indefinite judgment may dull the ethical sensitivity.

Still another force that changed the Christian movement
was Greek philosophy, with its emphasis on speculative
thought and its dualistic conception of life. The latter was
an integral part of some phases of Greek philosophy. Not
all the contributions of Greek thought to the Christian
movement were bad. Here, however, we are only attempting to discover some of the influences that contributed to
a changing Christian conception of the world which in turn
shaped Western civilization and helps to explain the contemporary crisis in the West.

Some of the early church leaders who were students of
Greek philosophy attempted to make the Christian religion
compatible with that philosophy. They became interested
primarily in the speculative phases of Christian theology.
Theology is an important phase of the Christian religion,
but too frequently Christian leaders have been more interested in the speculative than they have in the practical
aspect of the Christian life. Theology, of course, is not necessarily exclusively speculative; it may be quite practical in
its approach. We do not mean to belittle even the specu-

lative phases of theology, but we are seeking to emphasize that the outstanding weakness of historic Christianity, as of contemporary Christianity, was its moral or ethical weakness. This fact is definitely a part of the background of the contemporary crisis. If Christianity had been the vital factor in the world and in the lives of individual adherents that it should have been, it is doubtful that we would have the present crisis.

Mention was made also of the influence of the dualistic interpretation of life which was prevalent in some Greek philosophy; in Plato, and more particularly in Neo-Platonism. The mystical and sectarian groups were particularly influenced by this dualistic conception. They, following certain Greek philosophical thought, considered the material world as evil. If the world was evil, then the Christian should withdraw or escape from it. He was not obligated to save the world but to save himself and other individuals from the world. It can be seen easily that those holding to such a position would not contribute a great deal to the Christianization of civilization. While those who held to this position may have represented a decided minority, nevertheless, their attitude in general became rather prevalent among the rank and file of Christians of that day.

This correctly suggests that there have been conflicting trends within the church and within civilization. These conflicting trends have continued through the centuries and help to explain the modern crisis in the world.

THE UNIFICATION OF CIVILIZATION

A strong desire for unity seems to have been a part of the very genius of the Roman Empire and of its rulers. This desire for unity was one reason for the persecution of the

Christians by some of the Roman emperors. They considered Christianity as divisive, labeled it an illegal religion and tried to destroy it. Constantine, with a similar desire for unity, used a different strategy. He made the Christian religion, through the Edict of Milan in 313, a legal religion of the empire. It was placed at least on nominal equality with Judaism and paganism.

This strong desire for unity by Rome was carried over into the main stream of the Christian movement. The Roman Catholic Church, which was patterned after the empire, had such a desire and was as ruthless at times as the empire had ever been in its attempt to secure and to maintain that unity.

The Roman Church arose to power upon the ruins of the empire. As the political power became decadent and declined in prestige and influence, the so-called spiritual power became increasingly dominant. The Gelasian theory of the two swords became the accepted church position concerning the relation of the church and the state. The theory is that God has given to the prince the temporal sword, while to the priest he has given the spiritual sword. God has allotted to each his sphere of authority. Church authorities of the twelfth and succeeding centuries said that since the spiritual was superior, it followed that the secular or temporal rulers derived their authority from the church. They also suggested that since the spiritual sword was more important, it justifiably might control the temporal sword and demand that the temporal sword be used to promote spiritual ends.

This theory formulated by Gelasius in the fifth century has been the general position of the Roman Catholic Church concerning the relation of church and state through the centuries. At times other terms have been used to express very much the same idea. Hildebrand, or Gregory VII, the maker of popes and pope himself from 1073–1085, spoke of the relation of the church and state as the relation of soul and body. The church was the soul, which was certainly more important than the body.

This chapter is not a discussion of the relation of church and state, but this basic theory of the Roman Catholic Church was an important factor in the unification of a civilization.

The Roman Catholic Church became a temporal power of considerable influence when Pepin (or Pippin) the Short, of France, in 755 gave to the pope the civil control of Rome and the central part of Italy. The "papal states" were governed by the popes for approximately 1100 years.

In 774, Charlemagne recognized the pope's temporal power over "the papal states." In turn, Pope Leo III (795–816) in 800 conferred on Charlemagne the title of "Roman Emperor." Thus was born the "Holy Roman Empire." Charlemagne passed laws requiring that those who refused to accept Christianity should be put to death. The spiritual sword and the temporal sword were thus in the same hand.

Civilization was possibly more completely unified from the days of Charlemagne and the establishment of the Holy Roman Empire to the Reformation than at any other time. In the main, there was one dominant language—Latin; one dominant type of economic life—feudalism; one dominant political power—the Holy Roman Empire; and one dominant church—the Roman Catholic Church. There was a close affiliation of the church with every phase of the culture, and one could correctly say that, to a considerable degree, the church dominated all areas of life. This control or dominance was even extended to the lives, the minds, and the consciences of men.

To win and to maintain its power, the Roman Catholic Church used worldly methods, became a worldly power, and hence lost, to a very large degree, its spiritual power. Walter Horton [6] quotes Lord Acton, a Catholic, as saying that all power is corrupting, and that absolute power is absolutely corrupting. Horton concludes that "the nearest thing to absolute power in the Middle Ages was the power of the popes."

We have not sought to trace all the forces that contributed to the unification of civilization under the influence and dominance of the Roman Catholic Church. One group, however, made a distinctive contribution. They were the scholastics, particularly Thomas Aquinas, the greatest of the scholastics. This group attempted to weld together into one consistent whole Christian theology and Greek philosophy. The theology of Aquinas was built upon the philosophy of Aristotle. He did not see any necessary conflict between the natural (the area of philosophy) and the supernatural (the province of theology). The former provided the foundation, the latter the superstructure. One wonders how much scholasticism, with its emphasis on Greek thought, prepared the way for the revival of humanism in the days of the Renaissance.

The civilization that was unified, largely under the power and pressure of the church, is frequently pictured by Roman Catholic authorities as the golden age, not only of the church but of civilization. However, that unification carried within itself its own seeds of destruction. Any unification attained as it was, and particularly maintained by force as it was long after what inner unity and cohesion it had was gone, was doomed to collapse. Civilization became stagnated. Some drastic change was inevitable.

[6] *Op. cit.*, p. 87.

FRAGMENTATION OF CIVILIZATION

By "fragmentation" is meant the same thing that Berdyaev means by "decentralization." [7] This fragmentation, which, as suggested previously, was inevitable, took place during the days of the Renaissance and the Reformation. These two movements were merely different expressions of one general attempt to break out of the artificially maintained unity of civilization and to free the minds and creative energies of men from the enervating control of a decadent church. It is true that there were distinctive emphases in the Renaissance and the Reformation, which will be considered later, yet the two were parts of one general movement.

We are not concerned here with a comprehensive study of the Renaissance and the Reformation, but merely with a consideration of some of the phases of the period that will give us a background for an understanding of the contemporary crisis. The main thing, from the viewpoint of our particular interest, is that the old unity was broken up or fragmented. Politically, independent nations displaced the decadent Roman Empire. Economically, capitalism replaced feudalism. Intellectually, humanism challenged the authority of the Roman Catholic Church. Religiously, the reformed group broke away from the Catholic Church. The fragmentation of the more or less unified but decadent civilization released tremendous creative powers along these and other lines. It ushered in a new type of civilization which Sorokin [8] calls sensate—a civilization which emphasized primarily sensory values. In its early stages this sensate

[7] Nicholas Berdyaev, *The Meaning of History* (London: Geoffrey Bles, 1936), p. 130.
[8] *The Crisis of Our Age*, p. 20.

culture acknowledged its indebtedness to basic moral and spiritual principles and exhausted itself and became decadent only when it divorced itself from its moral and spiritual roots.

Although the Renaissance and Reformation freed the minds and creative energies of men, this did not mean that there were no claimants for authority over men and their affairs. During the period a struggle began over which of three conceptions would decide the final source of authority for man. This struggle has continued until today.

The Roman Catholic Church claimed, and still claims, that it is the final source of authority for men and their institutions. Protestantism, in the main, claims that the Bible is that final source, while humanism considers human reason as authoritative. For humanism the source of authority is within man; for Protestantism it is in a divine revelation; while for Roman Catholicism it is in a divine institution. The history of Western civilization for the past five centuries could be written around the conflict and the interplay of these three. We should remember, however, that the line of demarcation between Protestantism and humanism is not always sharply drawn; they have much in common. Protestantism, in the main, believes that the source of authority is exterior to man; that it is centered in the will of God. Protestants believe that the Bible is the revealed will of God, but they do not believe that the Bible is a rule book in which one can find a specific answer for every question of life. The Bible has to be interpreted and applied. Believing in the priesthood of every believer, they contend that the individual child of God has the right and the responsibility to read, to interpret, and to apply the Bible to his own life.

Some may contend that these views or beliefs of Protestantism are not different from humanism. While it is admitted that there is some similarity, yet, if properly understood, it will be seen that they are poles apart. Humanism says that the source of authority is within man, that man is competent to decide for himself what is right and wrong for him. It represents a purely rational approach to life and its problems.

Protestantism, when it has not been influenced too much by humanism, holds that the source of authority is exterior to man. God, rather than man, is the point of reference for all of life. The supreme question is not, What would right reason dictate, but, What is the will of God? And although Protestantism would claim that the individual Christian, rather than the Christian group or the church, should decide what is right for him, it will frankly admit that man, as man, is prone to err. He cannot trust unquestionably his reason or judgment. In seeking to know and to interpret God's will for his life, he should humbly admit his limitations and his need for the leadership of the divine Spirit.

This struggle concerning these opposing views of authority furnishes some of the background for the contemporary crisis. The struggle has been not only a contest for authority over man, but also a conflict within the soul of man himself.

SUBSEQUENT DEVELOPMENTS

The movements arising out of the Renaissance and the Reformation period have largely shaped the Western world since that time. The directions in which those movements developed are important background factors producing the contemporary crisis.

It has been implied previously that art and science, business and politics, all of which are closely related to and dependent upon religion, tended, at a comparatively early period, to assert too strongly their freedom from all moral and spiritual restraints. There developed an attitude of "art for art's sake," "science for science's sake," and "business for business' sake." Such attitudes meant that these areas of man's life claimed freedom from all external controls. As a result, men in these different phases of their lives have lost, to a large degree, any sense of responsibility to any law or authority outside themselves.

Many of the failures and problems in modern art and science, business and politics, as well as in other areas of the life of Western man, are due to this divorcement of so much of his life from God and from the authority of the basic laws of God. A sense of stewardship and of responsibility to God and to society has been lost largely. Since a common source of authority is lacking, there is no unity of purpose. The various realms of life are frequently in conflict and competition with one another. Also, separating themselves from divine resources, they have tended to exhaust the springs of their own creativeness. The world is reaping in the contemporary period some of the ultimate results of a culture which has divorced itself from its spiritual resources, a culture that has attached supreme value to the sensory rather than to the spiritual values of life.

Much could be said concerning the growing independence of various phases of the life of the world. Particularly pertinent for a study of the contemporary crisis would be a consideration of the developing independence of the capitalistic economic system and of political democracy. Each of these movements received much of its early impetus and inspiration from the Protestant movement. For example, some scholars consider the Protestant movement in general, and Calvinism in particular, as a major factor in the rise and growth of capitalism, especially industrial capitalism.[9]

While the contribution of Protestantism to democracy was not so immediate as it was to capitalism, it ultimately was just as great. Particularly important was the recapture of the dignity and worth of the individual and the attendant emphasis on the priesthood of the believer. Although the reformers themselves were not in practice very democratic, yet some of their principles, along with those of humanism, provided most of the ideas which later gave birth to the democratic movement.

A matter of particular interest to us is the fact that both of these movements, capitalism and democracy, which were so heavily indebted to Christian principles, asserted at a comparatively early period their independence of their Christian roots. The values which these movements fostered became for many people superior to the spiritual ideas and ideals which had so largely given them birth.

This latter trend we see particularly in the economic area where the material values have become the supreme values for millions of people. The good life has tended to be measured in material terms. Progress is determined largely in terms of improved gadgets, increased income, and better working conditions.

The same thing has happened in the political area. The political philosophy of democracy has tended to become an end independent of its religious base. One source for the ills of our nation and our world is this general divorcement of economic and political life from the moral and religious foundations of those areas of life.

[9] See R. H. Tawney, *Religion and the Rise of Capitalism*. A historical study. (Holland Memorial lectures, 1920), (New York: Harcourt, 1926), and Max Weber, translated by Talcott Parsons, *The Protestant Ethic and the Spirit of Capitalism* (London: George Allen and Unwin, Ltd., 1930).

Reference has been made previously to the place of humanism in the period of the Renaissance and the Reformation and its contribution to Western civilization. The humanism of the Renaissance and the Reformation era, in the main, was theistic. However, humanism gradually became anthropocentric rather than theocentric. It may be that such a shift was more or less inherent in the very nature of the movement. Humanism so exalted man that it was more or less inevitable, sooner or later, that he would be exalted to the place properly belonging to God.

Mention has been made of the fact that humanism and Protestantism have some things in common. The past four hundred years have been referred to as the Protestant-humanist era.[10] Both movements placed a high value on the human personality, although their appraisals were somewhat differently based. It seems that it was more or less inevitable that humanism would influence considerably the Protestant movement. This influence was particularly pronounced in theological liberalism. Some of the liberals, at least those of a generation or two ago, so exalted man and so played down the seriousness of sin and the need for divine intervention in the affairs of men that their theology became little more than theistic humanism.

Thus humanism as a movement, and also through its influence on liberal theological thought, is an important phase of the background for the modern crisis.

THE CONTEMPORARY SCENE

The contemporary scene was described, to a degree, in the first chapter. A brief statement here will suffice. The

[10] Paul Tillich, *The Protestant Era* (Chicago: University of Chicago Press, 1948), p. 274.

contemporary situation is hard to describe, even in broad outlines, without touching on the reasons for the crisis, which are reserved for a later chapter. It is also difficult to describe the contemporary scene because we are in the midst of it. It is difficult for us to know what is going on and even more difficult for us to interpret objectively and accurately what we do observe.

The increasing independence of the areas of life previously discussed is one characteristic of the contemporary scene. In every phase of his life man has refused, to a great extent, to acknowledge any source of authority external to himself, which has robbed him of his sense of the eternal. When robbed of the sense of the eternal, man loses the source, not only of his creativeness, but also of his stability and strength.

In losing, to such a large degree, a sense of the eternal and of a source of authority beyond themselves, art and science, business and politics have lost to a distressing degree a sense of stewardship. They have become ends within themselves when they should merely be means or methods. This is a part of the general transvaluation of values that plagues our world.

We are awakening to the fact that art, economics, politics, and particularly science may be used to destroy man. This will be true if the values within these areas become the ends for which men live, and thus lead men to divorce themselves from God and from a sense of responsibility to God and to society for what they do with the discoveries and advances they have made in these and other areas.

Standing at the center of the contemporary scene is man. The crisis of our world is basically a crisis concerning man and within man. We are reaping in the modern period the ultimate results of a nontheistic humanism which divorces man from God, denying that man is made in the image of God or is dependent upon God. When man exalts himself to the place that properly belongs to God, such exaltation really debases and dehumanizes him. Being divorced from the spiritual center of life, an exhaustion of his creative powers inevitably follows. It also follows that he tends to direct his attention to the periphery of life rather than to the center of life; to the things of life rather than to the ends of life. This is one of the chief problems of our day.

Recent events have disillusioned modern man. Because he has failed to solve his problems, he faces the possibility of his house collapsing on his head. He has broken, in the main, with the eternal springs of hope and renewal. He is a frustrated individual stricken with fear for the future and with a strong sense of futility. In the geographic areas where the contemporary disintegration has gone the furtherest, it is no wonder that man, seeking a renewal of meaning and significance of life, has turned to the superman of Nietzsche or to the collectivism of Marx.

It now seems that modern man will lean upon some power outside himself for security, for a sense of dignity and well-being. Many even want to "escape from freedom." [11] They are willing to surrender their liberty for security, with the hope that they will discover a new meaning in life. The next few years will determine whether man will turn to a political totalitarianism such as fascism or communism, to an ecclesiastical totalitarianism, or to a vital type of Christian experience. The latter alone will re-create within him springs of hope and a sense of personal responsibility that is needed in this day. A renewal of the image of God within, of a sense of dependence upon God but also a sense of partnership with a sovereign, ultimately trium-

[11] Tillich, *ibid.*, p. 286.

phant God, will release new creative powers within man and will save his soul from enslavement to the group or collective.

On the basis of a proper understanding of what has happened and is happening to man, we can understand, interpret, and evaluate the modern movements that challenge our accepted ways. On the same basis, we can better understand what has happened to our culture to make it so vulnerable to attack. From the same viewpoint, we can see more clearly the background for, and understand the direction of, modern theological and philosophical movements.

3

PHASES OF THE CRISIS

THE general thesis of this book is that the contemporary crisis is basically spiritual. If it is spiritual in the deepest and broadest sense, it will affect inevitably every other phase of life. Every area of life, in a very real sense, has a spiritual foundation or a theological base. That foundation or base may be sound or unsound, but, whichever it is, the shape and stability of the superstructure will be determined by it.

At the heart of the modern crisis is a struggle toward a new unification of life. The fragmentation of civilization which took place during the Renaissance and Reformation has run its course. While it led to tremendously creative movements, those movements, as suggested previously, asserted their independence too strenuously and failed to recognize the sources of their strength. Because they divorced themselves from the moral and spiritual resources that had given them birth and early vitality, they have exhausted largely their creative resources. The struggle to recapture the springs of youthful vitality and creativity is an integral part of the contemporary crisis in economic, political, and even in religious life. If it is correct that the present crisis represents a struggle toward such a new unification or integration of civilization, then naturally every phase of civilization will be involved in the crisis and will be affected by it. This will be just as true of science, art, and philosophy as of the areas specifically discussed in this chapter.

It also has been emphasized previously that the present crisis is comparable in seriousness to the period of the Renaissance and the Reformation. If this is correct, then every phase of civilization will be involved in and influenced by the crisis. If we are to judge by history, then there will come out of the contemporary crisis a new way of life in every area. In this chapter only three of these areas will be considered—the economic, the political, and the religious or spiritual. These realms are broad enough that they will touch directly or indirectly on every other phase of man's life.

We shall consider how each of these broad areas is involved in the modern crisis and what seems to be the direction in which the new order, now in the process of being born, may move in those areas. We shall give some attention to each as an element in the crisis and some contributions that may be made in each area to the solution of the crisis. The religious phase will not be treated here as thoroughly as the other two phases of the crisis since it will be considered at greater detail in later chapters.

ECONOMIC PHASES

Some people contend that not only is our economic condition a contributor to the crisis but that it is the chief fac-

tor in creating the crisis. Those who take such a position
insist that any adequate solution for the crisis must be primarily economic in its emphasis. Most, though not all, of
those who take this rather extreme position are economists.
They approach the problems of our society largely, if not
exclusively, from the economic viewpoint. For example, Eugene Staley's [1] general position is that the modern crisis
represents a conflict between a trend toward international
co-operation in the economic area and a trend toward nar-
rowing nationalism in the political realm. While these more
or less conflicting trends were more evident in the days of
World War II and the years immediately preceding than
they are today, they are still present and are factors in the
contemporary crisis. But it would be an oversimplification
to suggest this conflict as a chief cause of the modern crisis.

Other students of world affairs suggest that the economic
is *a* major factor although not necessarily *the* major factor
in the contemporary crisis. For example, Walter Lippman,
one of America's most discerning newspaper columnists, in
a book that was written before World War II (1937) but
which was printed in a new edition during the war (1943),
concludes that the central problem of the Western world
is the reconciliation of the division of labor, necessitated by
the industrial revolution, and the basic moral and religious
conviction "that all men are persons and that the human
person is inviolable." [2]

We should not shrug this off as of little consequence.
Lippman's thesis does pose a real problem and one that is
an element in the present crisis. Specialization and the division of labor in modern industry have been carried so far

[1] Eugene Staley, *World Economy in Transition* (New York: Council
on Foreign Relations, 1939).

[2] Walter Lippman, *The Good Society* (Boston: Little, Brown & Co.,
new edition, 1943), p. xi.

that relatively sharp class lines have been drawn. When these lines lead to clear-cut class consciousness, the foundations of our way of life are threatened. Some people tend to consider others as members of a certain class rather than as members of the human race. Such an attitude contributes to a breakdown of respect for human personality as such. No element in our Western way of life is more fundamental.

It is possible, however, to have class divisions within society without the class consciousness that undermines the foundations of our way of life. There is a difference between a classless society and a society that is not conscious of class divisions. It seems to be impossible to have a classless human society. There are of necessity racial, cultural, and economic classes. Even Soviet Russia, which theoretically has attempted to develop a classless society, has discovered that modern industrial life requires a division of labor. We can have no division of labor without some division into classes.

The only way for human society to be saved from self-destructive class consciousness is for it to have a deep sense of human dignity and brotherhood. A brotherhood that will cross over every class line is impossible apart from a deep consciousness that men are made in the image of God and are actual or potential children of God and hence brothers or potential brothers in the family of God.

This is one reason why communism is a false hope. It theoretically contends for a classless society, which is an impossibility, particularly in a highly industrialized society. On the other hand, communism does not have the spiritual resources to build a society that is not conscious of class. The latter can be done only within a Christian fellowship; and, incidentally, the Christian movement has not done a very good job along that line.

Possibly one other thing should be said concerning the economic class divisions that have contributed to the crisis of our day. These divisions become more acute as the peoples of the different classes become increasingly materialistic. In other words, the more the economic becomes the main concern of the people, the sharper are the economic class lines drawn and the deeper becomes the consciousness of class distinctions.

The past century has been called the century of economic man. Economic interests have become the prevailing interests of the majority of the people. The materialistic spirit has permeated all of life, including the field of organized religion. "Modern man is the product of a fervid obsession with material and social progress, with the gospel of more and more things." [3] Man's obsession with the things of life contributes not only to the deepening of class consciousness, but it also contributes in other ways to the tensions and problems of the contemporary period. Modern man's desire for things material has been fed by the system under which he lives, a system which has definitely an economic orientation. These materialistic desires are not easily satisfied. They are factors in the rise of contemporary economic and political movements and programs, such as communism, fascism, socialism, and even New Dealism. These movements have appealed to, and some have even taken advantage of, modern man's longing for economic security. We also should remember that "security" is not usually interpreted in terms of the necessities of life. "To the mass mind of today, the good life has become inseparable from the maximum consumption of things!" [4] Davies suggests

[3] D. R. Davies, The Sin of Our Age (New York: The Macmillan Co., 1947), p. 59.
[4] Ibid., p. 45.

that because the modern obsession with social security goes far beyond minimum physical needs, the problem has become social and spiritual more than strictly economic.

The high premium placed on material values and on economic security has created within man an inner conflict or dilemma. Man seems to have an inborn desire for freedom. But what is he to do when there is a conflict between freedom and economic security? "The most difficult thing is to unite bread and freedom. How can man be fed without taking from him his freedom?" [5] Unfortunately, millions of people seem willing to sell their birthright of freedom for economic security. Also unfortunate and yet ultimately encouraging is the fact that they cannot find the satisfaction which they are seeking by thus surrendering such a priceless heritage.

Can any society provide adequately for the economic needs and wants of its people and at the same time protect their liberties? It is doubtful if this can be done in an economically orientated society where profit is the chief motive and every conceivable means is used to stimulate artificially the economic wants and demands of the people. But there is no reason why it cannot be done within the democratic framework if we can have a reorientation of our thinking concerning the values of life. We must come to realize that the material values are not the supreme values of life, but that the moral and spiritual values are to have precedence.

We do not mean by this that the material things of life should be belittled. Certainly, we do not mean that religion should be the opiate of the people to lull them to senseless satisfaction with conditions they should not accept. We are simply saying that the material values should and must

[5] Berdyaev, *Towards a New Epoch*, p. 77.

fall into their proper place, which is a place subservient to the spiritual. This must be true not only of the laboring class but also of the middle and upper classes. The latter are the ones, in the main, who can create the conditions that will make it possible for society to provide both security and freedom.

It has been implied that Christians should not be too concerned about the name of the economic system. We should remember that systems change internally. For example, what is called "capitalism" today is considerably different from the capitalism of twenty-five or fifty years ago. The same can be said of "communism" as found in the Soviet Union.

We should be more concerned about what the label really means to human beings and to the moral and spiritual values of life than we are with the label itself. The good economic system is the one that is good for men and women, for their basic institutions, and for the kingdom of God among men. Possibly it should be added that no system is entirely good. We should not identify the kingdom of God with any particular economic system. Only a church that does not identify itself with a particular economic order can lift that order toward the Christian ideal.

Really, if we examine carefully existing economic systems, we shall discover that there is no pure system. Every country in the world has a mixed system. It is correct, however, to say that the struggle between capitalism and competing systems is a factor in the present crisis. That struggle is not only a struggle between systems, but also a struggle within those systems. The ultimate results of the struggle will be a factor in determining the shape of the economic order of the future. Particularly acute at the present time is the conflict between communism and the ways of the West. Some consider the present crisis as primarily a result of this struggle. While we should not belittle communism and its challenge to the West, yet the rise of communism is as much an evidence of and a result of the crisis as it is a factor in it. Until we recognize this fact, we cannot oppose communism successfully.

In a very true sense the conflict between capitalism and communism is a conflict between competing materialistic regimes. One may be, as Charles Malik, the representative of Lebanon to the United Nations, says, a soulless materialism and the other a militant materialism,[6] but both are basically materialistic. This is one reason why communism does not offer a real solution for the more fundamental problems of the capitalistic system. The problems of contemporary capitalism stem from the wrong evaluation of values; from the exaltation of the material to the place that properly belongs to human and spiritual values. Communism not only does not solve this problem, but it actually deepens it by making the economic or material the determinative factor in all of life.

To be entirely fair, we should admit that not only is the challenge of communism to capitalism a result of, and yet a factor in, the crisis, but the same can be said also of the co-operative movement and of socialism. These movements also have challenged capitalism, and because they are not as extreme as communism, they possibly have influenced capitalism more than communism.

The capitalistic system is very vulnerable to attack because it has either created or has failed to solve some very serious human problems. If the leaders of the capitalistic system had applied the same intelligence and vigor to solv-

[6] Charles Malik, *War and Peace* (New York: The National Committee for Free Europe, Inc.), pp. 29–30.

ing these problems as they have to discovering new sources for raw materials and new markets for finished products and to increasing profits, they would have found a way to solve them.

Among the more important of the problems are: poverty in the midst of plenty; unemployment and depressions that seemingly cannot be reversed except by arming for war; and inequitable distribution of wealth and income. It should be stated again that capitalism has not necessarily created these problems. Really, we find less poverty and more wealth for all in the more strictly capitalistic, industrialized nations. Many feel, however, that there is too big a gap between what the system can and does produce and the share received by the people who furnish the brawn for the production.

Another factor of some proportions in the crisis is the struggle upwards of the underprivileged, backward nations and peoples. The have-nots are struggling to raise their status in the world. It seems that the more favored peoples of the world must be willing to share with the less privileged. In other words, there must be a leveling, to some degree, of the living standards of the different peoples of the world.

One contributor to these problems has been the materialistic spirit. If people were not so materialistic, they would not be so demanding. But who or what has made them materialistic? Has not the capitalistic system contributed to this spirit, a spirit that now threatens the system itself? This materialistic spirit has not only contributed to the crisis by creating a deepening dissatisfaction among the toiling, underprivileged masses, but it is also a factor in the crisis through its domination, to such a large degree, of the purposes and motives of those who control industry and business. If industry and business were not so predominantly concerned for increased profits, they might be willing voluntarily to share more equitably with those who toil with their hands and thus relieve one source of contemporary tension.

Some believe that a major element in the struggle within the economic area is the movement toward a planned economy. For example, Karl Mannheim says: "There is no doubt that our society has been taken ill. What is the disease, and what could be its cure? If I had to summarize the situation in a single sentence I would say: 'We are living in an age of transition from laissez-faire to a planned society. The planned society that will come may take one of two shapes: it will be ruled either by a minority in terms of a dictatorship or by a new form of government which, in spite of its increased power, will still be democratically controlled.' " [7] Mannheim and others contend that some type of planned economy is to be characteristic of the new world order that is struggling to be born. The only unanswerable questions, from their viewpoint, are the purposes for which the planning is to be done, the degree of planning, and who is to do the planning.

Whether or not the preceding is correct, we now have, and doubtless will continue to have, more or less planning in every major nation of the world. It now seems that what we shall have for the indefinite future is a mixed economy— part free and part controlled or planned both within the different nations of the world and on the international level.

Nobody knows the exact shape of the economic order of the future. Stuart Chase speaks of it as "X, the unknown." In speaking of the new system that is rising, he says, "Some-

[7] Karl Mannheim, *Diagnosis of Our Time* (New York: Oxford University Press, 1944), p. 3.

thing has appeared which nobody anticipated, nobody wanted and nobody really understands." [8]

Chase asks why can we not recapture the system which proved itself a good system and one which is still preferred by most of the leaders of the United States and Britain. His answer to his own question is: "Because the basic conditions which made it a good and workable system for a century and more, have so changed that it has now become unworkable over great areas." [9] The conditions that have made some changes necessary are factors in creating the crisis.

POLITICAL PHASES

The economic and political phases of the contemporary crisis are interrelated. For example, one phase of the present crisis is the struggle between the economic and the political to determine which will be dominant. The economic has been, and for millions of people it still is, the dominant interest of life. It is also true that the economic has largely controlled the political. Governments have been controlled by particular economic classes and used to promote the interests of those classes. The governments of the world, in the main, are attempting now to control economic life and, theoretically at least, to make the economic order serve the best interests of the nation and of the people as a whole. This is a part of the movement toward a planned or controlled economy mentioned previously. If we are to judge by modern trends, such a control of the economic by the political is among the inevitables of life.

[8] Stuart Chase, The Road We Are Traveling, 1914–1942 (New York: The Twentieth Century Fund, 1942), p. 95.
[9] Ibid., p. 94.

Other political phases of the contemporary crisis that are not related so closely to the economic, although they have definite economic implications, are the minorities and immigration problems. Both are worldwide in scope and are factors in creating the tensions of the present time. They pose a real question for those who are interested in building a world that is unified politically.

These political and cultural minorities are found in most countries of the world. They are the restless and, from their viewpoint, the disinherited of the world. As they become articulate in their dissatisfaction, they will become an increasing factor in the present crisis. This is particularly true as they join hands with minority groups of other nations and sections. Some groups, such as the colored peoples, are not numerical minorities, but they make common cause with the minorities because, to such a large degree, they are among the have-nots of the world.

On the question of the immigration problem, there is persistent pressure for "living room" to ease the crowded living conditions of the more densely populated areas of the world. In the main, these areas are populated by the colored peoples. On the other hand, the Caucasians have been particularly restrictive and discriminatory in limiting immigration from the areas under the greatest pressure. There is increasing sentiment for a free movement of peoples anywhere in the world. This seems to be unrealistic for the time-being, but we must admit there is no easy solution to the immigration problem.

Another problem is the awakening of the colonial peoples of the world. This awakening is of considerable importance in the contemporary crisis. It has resulted, to a considerable degree, from the appropriation by the colonial peoples of some of the basic moral and political ideas and ideals of the Western world. As those peoples have become more mature politically, they have used the ideas of the West to challenge the right of those who rule over them to continue such rule. This challenge has not only been a direct factor in the tensions of the contemporary period, but it has also contributed indirectly to the crisis by being a factor in the shifting power positions of the major nations of the world.

This shifting is a part of, and a contributor to, modern political dislocation. For example, the decline of Great Britain as a world power cannot be understood apart from the partial breakup of her vast colonial empire.

We cannot understand the present crisis unless we sense the deep striving going on within the soul of the world for unification. This involves, among other things, political unification. It seems that a new world order is struggling to be born and that one characteristic of that new order will be some kind of unified world government. Arnold Toynbee, the world renowned English historian, has expressed the idea as follows: "I believe it is a foregone conclusion that the world is . . . going to be unified politically in the near future. . . . I think the big and really formidable political issue to-day is, not *whether* the world is soon going to be unified politically, but in which of two alternative possible ways this rapid unification is going to come about." [10] Toynbee gives two major reasons for the inevitability of political unification: the degree of our present interdependence and the destructiveness of the modern weapons of war. The two methods of unification, according to Toynbee, are by force or by co-operation. Wars may continue, and likely one more would be sufficient, until just one great power would survive, which would impose unification and peace upon the

[10] *Civilization on Trial*, p. 127.

world by force of arms. This has been done in the past. The only other method, which does not look encouraging now, is through the co-operation of the nations of the world, particularly the two great world powers—the United States and the Soviet Union. Such co-operation might require limited surrender of sovereignty by every nation, but it is possible that the nations would gain much more than they would lose.

Where does the United Nations fit into this general picture? If the world is struggling toward some type of effective world government, then the United Nations may represent a step in that direction. It is increasingly evident, however, that the United Nations is not the ultimate answer in world government. The United Nations as it now exists has some of the same weaknesses as the League of Nations—weaknesses that meant that the League failed in times of emergency. At best the United Nations, as was true of the League, is merely a conference of sovereign nations. The major nations of the world, as in the case of the League, are not willing to give any real power to the United Nations. It has a "military staff committee," but so far this committee is the extent of its military establishment. It lacks the police force to enforce its decisions on the nations of the world.

We are not belittling the work of the United Nations. It has done well under the circumstances, but its limitations, which were established and are maintained by the major powers, have contributed to the mounting tension and sense of crisis in the world. The peoples of the world who want peace see no chance that the present world political setup can stop an aggressor nation without resorting to the old method of other nations meeting force with force. Regardless of how much we may try to make it appear otherwise, this is what happened in Korea. The first action there was by the United States, and then later some of the nations within the United Nations came to the assistance of the United States by volunteering token forces.

If the peoples of the world could decide, if they were wise and logical, they would vote for an effective world government with enough police power at its command to maintain order in the world. Likewise, if the small nations could determine world policy, and if they were wise, they would vote for such a world power. It is only within such a framework that they can have any real freedom. Of course, whether or not they would have freedom under a world government would be determined by the type of government established.

One other statement should be made concerning the trend toward the political unification of the world. If such a political unification is an integral part of the new world order that is in the process of being born, as implied by Toynbee, then the world will not get beyond the present period of chaos and confusion, of travail and suffering until the new order with its political unification is born. Once we are persuaded that this is to be a characteristic of the new order, then the quicker our nation and the other nations of the world recognize that fact and co-operate in the establishment of an effective world government, the sooner will the world get beyond the present period of suffering.

A word of caution may be in order. While it seems that some type of international government is inevitable, we should not place too much faith in such a political instrument. Political unification may be an essential part of any adequate solution for the problems of the world, but we must remember that the ills of our world are basically spiritual. After all, the maladjustments and evils of the economic and political areas stem largely from moral and spiritual decay.

Also, we should remember that political unification could deepen our problems, particularly if that unification were achieved and maintained by force. We could have the most completely totalitarian regime that the world has ever known. There could be a world political power allied with, or even controlled by, a world religious power that would seek to dominate even the minds and consciences of men. We could have a new Dark Ages. We should never forget that "sinful men will pervert any form of organization." [11] It is Christianity's business to do something about sin and sinful men.

The implication has been that the great powers, in the main, are the ones that are hindering the attainment of a new political order. Certainly the United States is one of those great powers. If we are correct in our diagnosis, then the United States is involved in the crisis. Some of the mistakes that our nation has made in the past have contributed to the present crisis. Although we have been freer than other major nations from imperialistic motives, nevertheless, our skirts are not entirely clean. We at least have used our economic resources and our political power to impress and influence the peoples of other nations. This has been a reason, along with an element of jealousy, for their dislike of us. While this dislike is not universal, it has become general enough to make it hard for our nation to exercise the moral leadership it should have in the world.

Also, our bungling, vacillating foreign policy has been a factor in the present crisis. Too frequently our leaders have demonstrated how to alienate friends and not to influence

[11] The Archbishop of Canterbury in *Towards a Christian Order* (London: Eyre and Spottiswoode, Ltd., 1942), p. 9.

people. We, the greatest democracy in the world, frequently have found ourselves defending old regimes of other nations that were doomed to die. The United States, more than any other nation of the world, should have a sympathetic understanding of the desire of the restless masses for freedom and status. The capture of those masses, to such a large degree, by communism is a major element in the contemporary crisis. Trueblood sums up the situation as follows: "By our concentration on money or power and on 'containment' we have allowed our ideological competitors to pose as the idealists, seeking justice and liberation and land reform, while we have been made to appear as men devoid of a dream, seeking only to protect and maintain a high standard of material comfort." [12]

Not only the United States, but the democracies in general are deeply involved in the present crisis. The failure of the democracies to apply consistently the democratic spirit and democratic principles is a factor in the crisis; and yet the spread of democratic ideas to the peoples of the world is also a factor in the crisis. It is a strange paradox of history that communism has stepped in and taken advantage of the failure of the democracies to apply consistently democratic principles.

If democracy is to contribute what it should to the release of the tensions of our day, it must come back to its Christian roots.[13] Toynbee suggests that democracy is a leaf from the book of Christianity which has been half emptied of meaning by being divorced from its Christian context and secularized.[14] Maritain similarly says that democracy "springs in the essentials from the inspiration of the gospel

[12] Trueblood, The Life We Prize, pp. 20–21.
[13] See Arthur E. Holt, Christian Roots of Democracy in America (New York: Friendship Press, 1941).
[14] Civilization on Trial, p. 236.

and cannot subsist without it." He then adds that for the
past century the motivating forces in modern democracy
have repudiated "the Gospel and Christianity in the name
of human liberty," while the "motivating forces in the
Christian social strata were combatting the democratic as-
pirations in the name of religion." [15] The latter has not been
true of all Christian forces, but it certainly has been true
of the dominant religious groups in most of the countries
of Europe.

Closely related to the preceding is the whole matter of
the relation of church and state and the attendant problem
of religious freedom. An adequate discussion of church and
state would require an entire book, or at least a separate
chapter. It is important, however, when the world is in the
process of bringing forth a new way of life, that people give
attention to the relation of church and state. Different in-
terpretations concerning the relation of the two and different meanings attached to religious freedom are contributors
to the tensions of the present period. We should remember
that it is important that these two divine-human institutions should be kept in proper relation to each other in any
new order that may arise. If this is not done, the world may
find that it has a new order but not a better one.

One of the most serious barriers to the achievement of
any effective world political unification is the sharp disa-
greement in theory and in practice concerning the relation
of church and state. The ideas concerning the proper relation of the two vary all the way from those who would
have one dominate the other to those who stand for a complete separation of church and state. Even those who contend for separation do not entirely agree. For example, the
Soviet Union maintains the separation of the church from

[15] *Christianity and Democracy,* p. 27.

the state and the school from the church. Although the communistic position today may be somewhat more liberal toward religion and the church than formerly, the basic theory remains the same. In other words, in the Soviet Union there is separation, but an unfriendly separation. It is based on the terms outlined by the state and thus means a domination of the church by the state.

On the other hand, in the United States there is a friendly separation, with each, the church and the state, recognizing that it has some responsibilities to the other. According to the American system and tradition, separation means an organizational and a functional separation, with the state protecting the right of the churches and the people to worship God according to the dictates of their own consciences. The church also has the right, under our interpretation of the proper relation of the church and state, to expect the state to protect it in the propagation of its faith. This right is denied to the church under the communistic conception of the relation of the two.

When we remember the large number of nations that maintain an established church and remember that the most liberal of these do not provide for complete religious liberty but merely for toleration, we can see some of the problems faced by any proposed world government. The real friends of full religious freedom must insist that this basic freedom be provided for all nations and peoples if a world government of the future is to receive the approval of the Christian forces. Such a provision would necessitate a separation of church and state. As suggested previously, there is a possibility of a unified political world which might form an alliance with a world ecclesiastical power and give the world the most completely totalitarian regime it has ever known.

RELIGIOUS PHASES

If the world is moving toward some form of unification, then inevitably every phase of life will be involved in that unification. This will be true within each phase of the civilization, but it will also be true within the civilization as such. In other words, there will be a struggle toward unification in the economic, political, religious, and other phases of the civilization, but there will be a struggle also toward a unification of all phases of the civilization around an integrated center.

Since there is a movement toward a new unification in the economic or political area, and particularly in the political area as stressed previously, then it is more or less inevitable that a similar struggle or movement will develop toward unification within the religious area. This is one possible explanation for the modern emphasis on the ecumenical movement. It is no mere accident that the formation of the World Council of Churches and of the National Council of Churches in America has taken place since World War II during the time when there also has been considerable discussion concerning the formation of a world political government. These movements within the religious area represent a part of the general movement toward unification.

While we shall not attempt here to judge the ecumenical movement, we should remember that many large Christian bodies have not as yet seen fit to identify themselves with the movement. They, along with others, believe that there is more than one way to attain meaningful spiritual unity. Such unity is possible without organizational union. Really, in the spiritual realm, as well as in the political area, premature organizational union may destroy the very unity that is desired. This poses a real problem in the area of political unification; for we can have no effective world organization until a world community is created. This condition is doubly true in the religious realm.

When we remember the major religious groups outside Christianity, such as Mohammedanism, Confucianism, Buddhism, and others, we begin to appreciate the difficulties that the world must overcome to create the spirit of brotherhood and of international unity that is necessary if the world is to have an effective international political organization. Such a spirit can be approximated only by the maintenance of the fullest religious liberty and the broadest tolerance and understanding.

The problem appears even more acute when we remember that communism is in a very real sense a religion and that it is the religion of millions of people. With its youthful vitality, it has become the chief challenger of Christianity. This challenge is a major element in the contemporary crisis.

We are not suggesting that there is no solution for this crisis, but we are saying that there is no easy way out of the crisis. Superficial remedies will not solve the problems of our world. This means, among other things, that a mere organizational reorientation of economic, political, and/or religious life will not go deep enough to solve the problems of the world or to relieve the tensions that have accompanied the contemporary crisis.

It is possible that some of the leaders in the ecumenical movement have thought of it as a method to revive the Christian movement and to recapture some of its lost prestige and power. However, the revival that is needed within the Christian movement is spiritual more than it is organizational. It will be tragic for the Christian movement and for the world if outer organization is substituted for repentance and inner spiritual renewal. It would be beneficial to the Christian movement and to the world if the Christian forces could make a united impact upon the world, but the lack of influence on the world by the Christian movement is not due primarily to its organizational weaknesses. Never before perhaps has the Christian movement had as many adherents, organized into as many strong churches, with as many beautiful buildings and well-filled treasuries. Never before have there been as many influential individuals identified with the Christian movement, nor as well-trained leaders directing the churches and the Christian movement in general.

The weakness of contemporary Christianity is not a lack of church members but the poor quality of church membership. The church's weakness is not a lack of material resources but of spiritual power. Many members of our churches make their relation to Christ and the church decidedly secondary. They do not make their love for Christ and their devotion to his cause the integrating center of their lives but place him at the circumference of life. What the churches need and what the world needs are more individuals who put Christ and his cause first in their lives. We must make our religion a living reality, a daily fellowship with and under the direction of the divine Spirit. This inner vitality must be recaptured by increasing numbers of church members if the Christian movement is to meet the challenge of the contemporary crisis. Until organized Christianity is thus revitalized, it not only will fail to meet the needs of the modern day, but it will be a contributing factor to the deepening of the contemporary crisis. Only a revitalized Christianity can provide the resources for the reorientation and reintegration of our civilization and our world.

4

FACTORS IN THE CRISIS

AS SUGGESTED previously, a crisis of the depth and breadth of the present one has many contributing factors. All these factors are interrelated, and while they evolve largely from a central or basic cause and are subsidiary to it, nevertheless, they are distinct enough to be treated separately. They deserve proper consideration, although they may be of secondary importance. In other words, the factors considered in this and preceding chapters are both causes and effects. While they are causes of the crisis, they themselves result from a deeper underlying cause. We can no more ignore these factors than we can ignore secondary causes in any other area of life.

WARS AND RUMORS OF WARS

In an earlier chapter we suggested that the present crisis was not a result of World War I and World War II but that these conflicts were an evidence and a result of the crisis. When a new way of life is being created, the transition period is characterized generally by chaos and confusion, struggle and travail, wars and rumors of wars.

This does not mean, however, that these wars have not contributed anything to the present world situation. While it is correct that they are primarily effects rather than causes, yet they are both causes and effects. The latter is particularly true if we take into account the constant threat of war since the close of World War II—a threat so real and accompanied by so much fighting that many people wonder if we are slipping from World War II into World War III without ever achieving world peace.

Add to this the threat of new and more terrible weapons of destruction, and one can readily see that wars and rumors of wars are real contributors to the crisis. Gripping the minds and souls of men is a terrible sense of uncertainty and tension. They are fearful that another war on a world scale may break out most any time and that such a war might mean the destruction of their homes, their nation, and their civilization. They are not sure that there would be a real victor in another war, and this thought has created in many a sense of urgency. They feel that something must be done to prevent another war and done quickly.

As man faces the problem of war in this modern day, he is aware of his inability to solve it. Man's voice is so weak, his strength so limited. What can people do in an atomic age? After all, they are not sure that those who are in places of leadership in the nation know what to do. And even if they did know, there are other nations that do not accept our standards. These nations might make it impossible for us to have peace.

A few people, such as the consistent pacifist, may think they have found the solution to the problem. At best, however, theirs is only a personal program. If they are realistic, they will admit that there are not yet enough people in the different nations of the world who would accept their solution to make it socially effective.

This sense of futility concerning war is a phase of the present situation. Remember we have suggested, over and over again, that this is a crisis within the soul of man. The sense of futility, which tends at times to plague the strongest and the best of men, is a part of this inner struggle.

The prevalence of a sense of futility helps to explain why so many men have turned to false saviors; to those who promise security and certainty, who promise to give peace and harmony. It has also been an element in the loss of faith of man in himself and in his ability to solve his problems and the problems of his world. He has come to realize that the disease is more serious than he had thought, and thus that the remedy must be more drastic than he had anticipated. His sense of futility will continue so long as he refuses to acknowledge his own limitations. He must discover that an adequate remedy for his problems must come from outside himself.

This may sound contradictory. We have suggested that man has lost his faith in himself, and yet he is unwilling to admit his limitations. It now seems that man is going to try to recapture his faith in himself by placing his faith in the group or the collective man. If the collective man—the party, the group, the race, or the nation—can solve man's problems, then he can retain or recover his "ego." Such a blind faith will merely deepen and prolong the present period of suffering. The problems of the present are basically spiritual, and, like the demons, they will come out only through much prayer and fasting. Spiritual problems demand spiritual solutions.

Wars and rumors of wars also have contributed to the present crisis in other ways. Two major wars within twenty-five years exhausted, to an alarming degree, the human and material resources of the central part of Europe where those wars in the main were fought. We need to remember that Europe was once the heart of Western civilization. But at the present time the geographic area which has been the creative center, not only of Western civilization, but to a less degree of civilization in general, has largely collapsed and lost its creativity. This is a factor of considerable importance in the present crisis.

It is also true that the extended preparation for war by the major world powers places such a strain upon the economy of those nations that it is a contributing factor to the crisis. This problem is particularly acute for the United States. It has to carry in addition to the load of its own armament program a considerable portion of the program for many other nations, including most of Europe. All this extensive financial program is threatening our nation with an inflation of such proportions that it will weaken our whole economy.

This simply means that war and the preparation for war are factors of considerable importance in the existing crisis. In a very real sense the world cannot solve the present crisis unless it can eliminate largely the possibility of another major world war. It does not seem that the latter is possible unless the nations of the world and the peoples of those nations discover the direction God is moving in the world and co-operate with him in bringing to birth the new world order that is now in the period of travail. It is a rather discouraging picture. Without a strong faith in a sovereign God, who cannot be defeated in his ultimate purposes, it would be a dark, forboding, if not a hopeless, picture.

SHIFTING POWER POSITIONS

Another factor of considerable significance in the present crisis is the shifting power positions of the major nations of the world. The wars of recent years, along with other forces, have caused this shifting. Before World War I there were several first-rate powers. At least the United States, Great Britain, France, and Germany would be considered in that category, with Russia potentially, if not actually, in that class. Japan was rapidly advancing. Italy, the low countries, the Scandinavian countries, the Balkans, and others were not so powerful, but they were strong enough to be respected.

A shifting of power positions followed World War I and during the years preceding World War II. Some nations, particularly Italy and Germany, set out on a definite program to recapture their lost prestige. A revolution took place in Russia that changed the complexion of the country. No one knew for sure how strong it had become until World War II. This war, in turn, revealed glaring weaknesses in some of the countries of Europe, particularly in France.

Coming out of World War II, the shifting of power positions was more evident than after World War I. As of the present, the only two first-rate powers are the United States and the Soviet Union. These two surpass to such a degree other nations in actual and foreseeable potential power that all other nations must be rated far down the line. Nations that were once proud and strong are now dependent for their very existence upon one of these great powers.

Such a situation is not a healthy one for world peace. This is particularly true when the two big powers are so far beyond the strength of any of the other nations of the world that no one of these smaller nations is powerful enough to serve as an effective balance. The United States and Russia have attained places of such dominance that the peace of the entire world depends on them. From the human viewpoint, one can correctly say that peace depends on either one.

These two powerful nations were at the circumference of the territory where World War I and World War II were largely fought. While both of them lost heavily in manpower, they did not feel the devastating effects of the wars as did the nations of Central and Western Europe. Some fighting was done on Russian soil, but not so much as in other parts of Europe. The destruction caused by these two wars in the heart of Europe has contributed to a shifting of power positions in Europe and in the world, and has also caused an economic and political dislocation that is an important contribution to this crisis period.

Europe had been for so long the center of Western civilization and a creative force in practically all cultures and civilizations of the world, it is possible that the decay, decline, and the collapse of her culture were major causes of the devastating wars of recent years. Even if this be true, those wars in turn have accelerated the decline in Europe.

It is possible that a decadent and senile Roman Catholic Church was, and is, a force in the decline of the culture of Europe. At least Roman Catholicism, which has been the dominant religion in much of Europe, has not had the vitality to check the disintegration and to change the direction of European civilization. There are some evidences that the decay in Europe has progressed furthest in the most predominantly Catholic countries.

Whatever may be the reasons for the disintegration and

threatened collapse at the very heart of Europe, it has created, to an alarming degree, an ideological vacuum in Europe. A vacuum, whether it is physical, ideological, moral, or spiritual, will not remain unfilled indefinitely. Part of the struggle between the United States and the Soviet Union, between democracy and communism, is an attempt to see which will fill that vacuum.

We do not mean to say that what happens in Europe necessarily will determine the destiny of civilization, but we do mean that what happens at the heart of Europe will color and shape the civilization of the future. At least, what is happening there is a factor in the present situation. The crisis will continue until a solution, more or less final, is found for the ills of Europe or until there is discovered a new creative center for Western civilization. The soundness of the solution or the validity and vitality of the new center would determine whether or not there would be any real and relatively permanent release from the chaos and confusion of the contemporary period.

Although Great Britain may not be of more importance than other nations of Europe, yet what happens to her is of particular interest to the United States. Once the mistress of the seas and the possessor of an empire on which the sun never set, the little island kingdom has seen its empire shrink and its grip on much of the remainder of the empire weakened. Gamely she is struggling now, not for a place of dominance among the nations of the world, but for actual survival. No one can calculate how much England's decline has contributed, not only to the sense of crisis in the world, but actually to that crisis.

So much has been said concerning Europe that one might conclude that the crisis stems entirely from the shifting power positions in Europe. But this is not the case.

We should remember that the Soviet Union is Asiatic as much as European. It never has identified itself fully with Europe and European culture.

The threat of communism is due partly to the fact that the backward nations, with their tremendous, undeveloped human and natural resources, are wide open for communist propaganda and infiltration. It is possible that the communist pressure in Europe kept the attention and interest of the leaders of the United States centered there while they took over in China. It may have been their plan all the while to move into the Orient, into countries that were made to order for their methods.

Through the conquest of China they have possession of a territory, if they can consolidate their position and exploit the resources, that will give them the greatest power potential in the world. Imagine what they will have if they succeed in taking over the rest of the Orient and then move into the Middle East!

Therefore, the threat of communism is of major importance in the present crisis. It may represent a shift of the power positions of some of the nations of the Orient as well as of the West. Time alone will reveal how far communism will move and how strong a force it will be in shaping the future.

SCIENCE AND THE MACHINE AGE

Science, through its contribution to the instruments of war, has also contributed to the shifting power positions of the nations of the world. Scientific progress along some lines is speeded up tremendously in times of war. The discoveries of science have made each succeeding war more destructive. The more destructive wars become, the more they contribute to a dislocation of all of life and to a general disintegration of the life and culture of the peoples involved. The more directly people are involved, the greater are the dislocation and disintegration.

No doubt the dropping of the first atomic bomb and the perfecting since that time of other and more devastating atomic weapons have been factors in creating the critical world situation. These developments represent a contribution of science to the crisis.

Science also has contributed to the present crisis by closing so largely the geographic frontiers of the world, and hence increasing the pressure within certain geographic areas. Science also has increased the tension among the different peoples of the world by making available to all nations the instruments of industrial production, thus increasing the competition for raw materials and for markets. Thus nations that were once consumer nations have become producer nations and competitors for the markets of the world. This has meant the shrinking of world markets, particularly for manufactured goods, and hence has contributed to increasing pressures within the more highly industrialized nations. This is one source of the problems of an island kingdom like Great Britain.

There are other ways that science has contributed to the crisis. It has made us "one world" or "one neighborhood." Those who were formerly around the world from us are now living in our back yard. Science has caused our world to shrink.

We are discovering that bringing nations closer together does not mean necessarily that they will get along better. It usually will mean one of two things: either a better understanding and a spirit of helpfulness or misunderstanding and a sharpening of conflict. If it is to be the former, there must be a genuine faith in one another or at least a conviction of the inherent worth of one another.

We also have discovered that science is impartial. It is neither good nor bad. It brings us closer together geographically, but it does not and cannot determine how we shall treat one another. It places within our hands its discoveries —discoveries that may enrich or impoverish, give life or death. Science does not determine the purposes for which it will be used. That decision is up to man.

The recognition of the power of science and of its limitations is a factor in the contemporary crisis. As suggested previously, it cannot determine the purposes for which it will be used. That is man's decision, and that is where the Christian religion comes into the picture. Christianity has a message for man and for the wills of men. It is the business of informed and consecrated Christian leaders to determine the purposes for which science shall be used. In other words, science cannot touch, at least directly, the motives, the ambitions, the desires, the purposes of men. That is the realm of religion.

One source of the troubles of our world is the fact that our religious knowledge, and particularly our religious fervor and practice, have lagged behind our scientific advance. As General Omar Bradley said, "Ours is a world of nuclear giants and ethical infants." Time alone will reveal whether man is going to have the depth of spiritual insight to use wisely what science has placed in his hands. Man has something in his hands with which he can destroy himself and his civilization. If he is wise, he will cry out, "Who shall deliver me out of the body of this death?" [1] The answer to that question will be found in the wisdom and power that come from the leadership of the Spirit of God.

[1] Rom. 7:24 ASV.

Science also has contributed to the crisis by creating the machine age. It has created the machines of war that threaten to destroy man and his civilization. It has provided the machines of production and also the instruments of communication that make available to the less industrialized nations these machines of production.

Our modern machines also contribute in a number of other ways to the present crisis. We shall limit our discussion here, however, to the machine's effects upon man. It has benefited man in many ways. It has lifted many burdens from his back. It has made life more livable. It has raised his living standards. It has enabled him to see further, to hear things he otherwise could not hear, to travel faster, and to fill his house with gadgets of all kinds.

The machine, however, is not an unmixed blessing. It has taken man away from nature. It has stepped between man and nature. It is conquering nature for man; but in conquering nature, it is also conquering man. The machine has liberated man, but it has also enslaved him.[2]

What has this enslavement of man by the machine done to him? It has contributed to his material-mindedness. Men who work constantly with machines tend to become a part of the machine. Their lives tend to be geared to the machine they operate.

Specialization has been carried to such extremes in modern industrialized life that work tends to lose its creativeness. One's task may be as simple and as monotonous as screwing on a certain nut on a machine as it passes. One of three things usually will happen to one who is thus tied down to the assembly line: (1) He will find a source for satisfying, creative living outside his workaday task at the club, fraternal order, or church; (2) or he will come to ac-

[2] Berdyaev, *The Meaning of History*, p. 152.

cept himself and his fellow workers as mere cogs in the industrial machine and of little more worth than the machines they operate; (3) or he may find himself continually dissatisfied, a ready object for rabble-rousers, Communists, or other disturbers.

We must acknowledge, of course, that all people are not working on the assembly line in some big industrial plant. This fact may be an element of hope in the entire situation. The trend, however, is toward the assembly line type of production in more and more areas of life. It is entering into the field of agriculture. Even some educational systems and institutions have approached the assembly line method.

In addition to this, the machine also has contributed to the crisis by making men so machine-minded that they can do no independent, creative thinking. They lack the intellectual equipment to meet the challenges of the day. They will either drift with the crowd or they will be led by men wise enough or, in most cases, shrewd enough to take advantage of their weaknesses. We have many evidences of such movements and leaders in recent years.

THE MARCH OF THE MASSES

No one can comprehend the modern crisis unless he understands that the masses are on the move. There is a stirring among the common people around the world. This stirring is important in the more highly industrialized nations, but it is far more significant in the less advanced nations where the masses are more or less constantly sick and hungry.

The march of the masses is both an evidence of, and an important factor in, the creating of the crisis. Every great revolutionary period is accompanied by, and in a sense is a result of, the rise of a new social or economic class. Some students of world affairs believe that just as the rise of the bourgeoisie resulted in or accompanied the displacement of feudalism by capitalism, also the rise of the working masses in our day is a forerunner of a new world order. Incidentally, it should be added that in the areas where the great majority of the underprivileged masses live, life is still largely feudalistic. Most of the land is owned by large landholders, while the masses are tenants—and tenants on a lower economic level than an American sharecropper can imagine.

History teaches that great world-changing movements come up from the masses, from the rank and file of the people. This is true of world-changing economic, political, and religious movements. Tensions and pressures within the underprivileged and disinherited masses seem to accumulate until a movement for release or for a revised status becomes more or less inevitable. When such a time arrives, the masses begin to march, and they will trample underfoot those who attempt to impede their progress.

This means that great world-changing movements are not the creation of the intelligentsia, of any individual, or of any small group of leaders. These may provide the ideas and principles that inspire world movements. The movements result, however, only when those ideas or principles have permeated the masses and created a restlessness within them. Movements create leaders more than they are created by leaders.

Social movements are somewhat like inventions. Every new invention is based upon many inventions that have gone before. When a certain inventive base has been built up, then a particular type of invention, which represents an advance, is more or less inevitable. The same thing is true of a social movement. When the base has been built up, not only through the pressure and tension within the masses but also in the total human experience, then the movement more or less inevitably follows. It would have come into being if a particular leader had never lived. For example, there would have been a Reformation if Luther had never been born.

What part, then, can and does the leader play in social movements? Is he merely a creation of them, an instrument or a means used by them? No, leaders can determine, to a degree, the speed with which movements will move and mature. They can shape those movements and can control and determine, to some degree, the purposes for which the movements will be used.

In any era when the masses are on the move, the place of leaders in the movements of the period will be determined by their rapport with the masses, their sympathy with the masses, and their co-operation with them. They at least have to give the impression that they are the champions of the people, that they are voicing for them the needs and purposes of their lives. This catching step with the marching masses helps to explain the influence of such divergent contemporary personalities as Stalin, Hitler, Mussolini, Gandhi, and Franklin D. Roosevelt. This fact also helps to explain the limitations of such dynamic personalities as Winston Churchill and Chiang Kai-shek. The latter men are not identified generally with the movement of the masses.

We do not mean to imply by what we have said that the movement of the masses is always and inevitably in the right direction. But we do mean that the masses are on the move around the world, in both the more advanced and in the backward areas of the world, in the East and in the West.

Frank Laubach, who possibly knows the mind of the masses as well as any living American, says of them: "They were in despair, but now they are making up their minds that they will come up—or blow up the world. They are desperate, grim, irresistible." [3] This he says is the crisis involving four-fifths of the world.

No longer are the masses gripped with a sense of sullen despair. It has changed to a desperate hope, a grim determination to come up out of their poverty and oppression. This new, grim determination and desperate hope are more or less inevitable by-products of their contact with Western civilization. Particularly important in stirring the sleeping masses has been the message of the missionaries. The Bible is the power of God, the dynamite of God. It has many interesting and meaningful by-products. Most of the elements in Western civilization that have stirred the minds of the underprivileged masses have come from Christianity. Particularly important at this point was, and is, the high value placed upon man, the dignity of the human person.

Whatever the source of the rise of the masses, this phenomenon is a major reason for the contemporary crisis. Berdyaev, as keen an analyst of the contemporary scene as any modern scholar, speaks of "the complete occupation of the stage of history by the mobilized masses." This he declares is "the basic factor of modern history." [4]

The Spanish philosopher, Jose Ortega y Gasset, suggests that the masses for the first time are taking seriously the basic principles or concepts of the democratic way of life.

[3] Frank Laubach, *Wake Up or Blow Up* (Westwood, N. J.: Fleming H. Revell Co., 1951), p. 28.
[4] *The Fate of Man in the Modern World*, p. 62.

He personifies the masses and speaks of the "mass man." For him, the mass man is a primitive man, rising up in the midst of the civilized world; he is like a spoiled child—ungrateful for all that has been done for him,[5] and has a deep desire to govern the world for himself.[6] While we may not agree entirely with Ortega y Gasset's diagnosis, believing that he is influenced too largely with the collapse of civilization in Europe, yet we can share his concern about the rising mass man, who has little place for a moral code and who claims to have rights but who is unwilling to accept the responsibilities those rights shall entail.[7] It should be remembered that the mass man does not belong to a particular economic or social class. He represents primarily a particular psychological attitude toward life.

Whether we use the term "the masses" or "the mass man," what is happening to the individual because of the rise of the masses is an element in the crisis. Several years ago, Albert Schweitzer said, "The modern man is lost in the mass in a way which is without precedent in history."[8] Let us remind ourselves again that the crisis of the individual in relation to the mass is not only a factor in the world crisis but also a result of that crisis.

The relation of the individual to the group or the mass in the modern period involves a paradox. As individuals among the masses have come to understand their personal dignity and worth, this understanding has contributed to the stirring among the masses which, in turn, contributes to the major social movements of the contemporary period.

[5] Jose Ortega y Gasset, *The Revolt of the Masses* (New York: W. W. Norton & Co., Inc., 1932), p. 63.
[6] *Ibid.*, p. 107.
[7] *Ibid.*, p. 201.
[8] Albert Schweitzer, *The Decay and the Restoration of Civilization*, p. 29.

On the other hand, these movements, at least as they have been shaped and controlled by self-seeking individuals and groups, have tended to swallow up the individual and to cause him to lose his sense of individual worth and even his individual identity. He seems to think that he can capture or recapture his sense of worth and dignity through the group. He usually finds, however, that the group exercises mastery over him and causes him to lose his sense of individuality and worth except as he identifies himself with the mass or the group. This paradox is one of the real threats to our world and is an important factor in the contemporary crisis.

It might be appropriate to direct a few words, at this stage of our discussion, to our churches and church leaders. First, they and we should remember that if our churches are to have an effective voice in shaping the future, in determining the direction in which the crisis is going to move, then they must maintain an effective ministry among the teeming millions around the world. These millions are hungry for light. They are marching, and many of them do not know where. They will follow those who will promise them bread, light, and love. The Christian movement can at least give them light and love, and it should be far more concerned than it has been in regard to their material needs. At least our churches and church leaders should be interested in seeing that they have the industrial and technical knowledge that would enable them to improve their status.[9]

The main thing for us to remember is that any Christian group that neglects the masses will not have an effective voice in the affairs of tomorrow. If our churches become

[9] See Willard R. Espy, *Bold New Program* (New York: Harper & Bros., 1950) which is the story of the famous "Point Four" program.

exclusively middle- and upper-class institutions that are uninterested in those who live across the tracks or down in the
flats, uninterested in the marching masses of China, India,
Africa, and the islands of the sea, then their days may be
numbered, and it may be later than we think.

Our interest in the masses, however, should not be a
selfish one. If we become interested in them simply to save
our own hides or to preserve our place in the affairs of the
world of tomorrow, such an interest will be self-defeating.
The masses will sense, sooner or later, our selfishness. We
should have a sincere interest in them simply because they
are men and women made in the image of God—men and
women for whom Christ died—men and women who are
just as valuable in the sight of God as the most educated
or the wealthiest. God is no respecter of persons, and we,
his children and his churches, should not be. This means
that we should minister to all, but we shall need particularly to guard against neglecting the disinherited masses.
It is so easy to neglect them. On the surface they have so
little to recommend themselves to our churches.

But these masses are on the march. Could it be that God
is on the march with them? If so, it would be doubly tragic
for us not to sense the direction in which they ought to
move and, to a degree, are moving and to catch step with
them and provide for them sufficient spiritual insight and
leadership to keep them from going in the wrong direction
or from being misled by those who would take advantage of
them by making promises to them that they cannot and
sometimes never expect to fulfil. Christian leadership certainly should never attempt to keep the masses in their
poverty. Even if we should attempt to keep them down, we
could not. Nothing can stop the upward move of the
masses. "This tide is as irresistible as the revolving of the

earth." [10] The glorious thing, however, is: "These helpless multitudes will follow anybody who tries to help them. You don't have to be educated; you only have to love." [11] This fact is glorious if the Christian movement will provide the leadership, but it may be terrible if communism provides the leadership. Communism, however, cannot provide leadership motivated by love. It is a creator of hate, and hate is ultimately self-defeating. Thus, ultimately, communism can offer no hope for the masses.

DECADENCE OF MORAL FOUNDATIONS

Whether we are thinking of our own nation, of Western civilization, of Oriental civilization, or of world civilization, another factor in the crisis is the decadence of moral and spiritual foundations. Trueblood concludes: "What we have is a *moral depression*." [12]

Every culture or civilization is based or built upon certain moral standards and ideals and/or theological concepts. For example, there is not only a theology of the Christian religion, but a theology of politics, [13] and a theology of economic life. For good or bad, certain theological concepts provide the background or the foundation for our so-called Western way of life. For instance, in this study we have referred a number of times to respect for human personality as foundational for Western civilization. This is fundamentally a theological concept, or at least it is based upon certain theological concepts.

Certain moral principles or standards provide the foun-

[10] Laubach, *op. cit.*, p. 58.
[11] *Ibid.*, p. 66.
[12] *The Life We Prize*, p. 37.
[13] See Nathaniel Micklem, *The Theology of Politics* (London–New York: Oxford University Press, 1941).

dation for our civilization the same as for any other definable culture or civilization. Those moral principles, along with the theological concepts, color and largely determine the nature of the civilization. The civilization is the superstructure that has been built upon these principles or concepts. Change the principles or standards which provide the foundation, and the superstructure will also be changed. The period of change or transition will be a period of confusion and crisis.

To say somewhat the same thing in another way, if the foundation becomes decadent, the whole superstructure will become decadent and will be threatened. Who would dare to say that the moral foundations of our way of life have not become decadent? The headlines of our daily papers will give adequate proof of the extent and depth of the decadence. The general picture in recent years has been rather sordid on "Main Street" and in our nation's capital. Just to record the words "divorce," "Kinsey Report," "Kefauver committee," "Fulbright committee," "mink coat," "tax collector," "cocktail bar," "gambling," "cribbing," "juvenile delinquency," "narcotics," and "homosexuality" is enough to call to mind recent revelations of the internal weaknesses of our nation. If the history of the rise, the decline, and the fall of nations and civilizations reveals anything, such moral conditions are among the surest signs of the threatened collapse of a nation or of a civilization. We assume that the situation in our nation is no worse than it is in other nations. If such an assumption is correct, then Western civilization is in a bad way and is seriously threatened.

The chief threat to any individual, family, nation, or civilization is inner decay rather than external pressure. Threats from without become serious primarily because of inner decay. "Once ethics are pushed aside, the foundations of human society begin to slip and slide." [14] The problems that arise in the economic and political areas are merely symptomatic of the inner condition of our way of life.

What are some of the reasons for this moral decay? There are many contributing causes. The breakdown of authority in the home is a major one, although the home should not be made the scapegoat for all the ills of our society. After all, how do we explain the breakdown of the home? Conditions in our homes are not only causes of the moral crisis we face, but those conditions are effects or results, to a degree, of influences outside the home. Every parent, however, should be deeply conscious of his responsibility to cultivate in his children respect for constituted authority and for those who exercise that authority. Through the home the children also should have built into the very fabric of their being basic moral principles—principles that will contribute to pure motives, to unselfish purposes, to strength for the storms of life, and to genuine integrity of character.

We do not have the space to consider the responsibility of the school, the state, and the church for the decadence of moral foundations. They, however, share that responsibility with the home. Also, the urbanization of life has contributed some to moral decay. The city tends to maximize indirect and secondary contacts and to minimize the more direct, face-to-face, primary relations. There is a relaxing of old controls, and so far there are no adequate substitutes.

Another reason for the inner moral weakness of our nation and of Western civilization is the fact that our nation and other nations have drifted so far from the basic moral

[14] Lewis Mumford, *Faith for Living* (New York: Harcourt, Brace & Co., 1940), p. 156.

principles or theological concepts such as the dignity and worth of the individual, which in turn is based on the conviction that man is made in the image of God. It is such principles or convictions that helped to give us birth and have sustained us and made us strong through the years. Our nation and other nations of the West continued for a considerable period to profess their adherence to these basic moral principles but practically to deny them in their lives. The results of such inconsistency are not particularly damaging so long as people admit that their lives do not measure up to their principles, so long as they repent of their sins and shortcomings and make an honest effort to measure up to their standards or ideals.

It should be remembered, however, that such a more or less hypocritical position cannot and will not be maintained indefinitely. Sooner or later our practices will affect our principles. Sinful, egotistic men and nations tend to justify as right what they continue to practice. They tend to develop what Trueblood calls "the easy conscience." [15]

The moral foundations of a nation or a civilization are seriously threatened once the people attempt to justify their sins and failures and adjust their ideals to their level of living. During the time while a civilization has cut itself loose from its moral foundations but still shows some of the fruit of those principles, we have what Trueblood has so aptly called a "cut-flower" civilization.[16] A cut-flower, separated from the source of its strength, may retain its beauty for a few days, but it soon withers and dies. Is Western civilization such a cut-flower civilization? If so, death is inevitable unless it recaptures its faith in the basic principles which have given it life and vitality.

[15] *The Life We Prize*, p. 63.
[16] *Foundations of Reconstruction*, p. 37.

We should remember that it is not just the mass man of Ortega y Gasset who aspires to live without conforming to any moral code. Europe in general and the world in general are without a moral code or at least without an accepted code outside themselves. "The leading classes have gone morally bankrupt." [17] This moral bankruptcy which affects every class of our society threatens our way of life. We must rebuild the foundations.

[17] Maritain, *Christianity and Democracy*, p. 75.

5

HEART OF THE CRISIS

AN UNDERSTANDING of all the contributing factors to the crisis is essential to a proper perspective concerning it. We have emphasized, however, that the contemporary crisis is basically spiritual, and in some way spiritual values are involved in every phase of it. This is just as true in the economic and political spheres as it is in the more strictly religious areas.

In this chapter we shall give, under several headings, particular attention to the heart of the crisis.

The heart of the crisis is so important that one has to look at it from different viewpoints to understand it or to get the proper perspective concerning it and its significance. These different viewpoints properly might be considered as merely various but integral phases of the real problem.

Still another way of approaching the whole problem is to say that the chief cause for the crisis in civilization is the weakening, the corrupting, the loss of vitality and virility of the integrating center of civilization, and that the secularization of life, the dethronement and humanizing of God, and man's loss of faith are factors in that disintegration.

DISINTEGRATION OF THE INTEGRATING CENTER

Every civilization has an integrating center around which that civilization is built. That center contains the supreme value or values of the civilization. It represents the ends for which men live and die. Those ends or ideas and ideals provide the point of reference for the civilization. Every phase of that civilization is related to and is subservient to that center. The values contained within that center are diffused through the entire civilization. Anything to which a civilization attaches supreme importance is really the religion of that civilization. Thus the integrating center of a culture or a civilization is its religion, although that center, and hence its religion, may be a false one.

Since this is true, it is of major importance that a civilization have a sound, a stable, a valid center. A false center might hold a civilization together for a while, but it contains within itself the sources of its own ultimate destruction and the destruction of the civilization unified around it.

It should be remembered, however, that a nation or a civilization that is thoroughly integrated around a false center may be able to compete successfully for a considerable period of time with another civilization that may be built around a sound or valid center, but whose life is not integrated so thoroughly. We have seen demonstrated in recent years, at least on the national level, the truthfulness of this statement. In other words, the strength of a nation or a civilization does not depend entirely upon the soundness of its integrating center, but also upon the thoroughness with which all the life of that nation or civilization is integrated around or held together by that center. Let us visualize this by thinking of that center as a giant magnet. If that magnet is not powerful enough, some areas of life, particularly out on the circumference, will not be held together by it.

Again we emphasize that the strength of a civilization will be determined largely by the inner unity or cohesion of the center itself. If disintegration begins within the center, then that center will lack the necessary vitality and virility to unify the various phases of the civilization.

Civilizations may decay and ultimately fall, either because of competition from without or because of inner disintegration. Of course, both of these sources of decay may be operative at the same time. The effects of a competing civilization will not be too serious on another civilization so long as only the techniques, the skills, or the means of the competitor are adopted. The threat becomes very real, however, when the ends or values of a competing civilization are accepted. When the latter happens, a reorientation of life around a new center begins, and a period of confusion is an inevitable result until a new center is established.

Western civilization is not threatened primarily by competing civilizations. The crisis within the West has resulted primarily from the weakness or decadence of its integrating center rather than from competing influences from without. Trueblood expresses this idea as follows: "The life we prize is seriously threatened, not primarily by any probability of attack from a foreign power, but by the battle of ideas within our own Western society." [1] It is a crisis within

[1] *The Life We Prize,* p. 36.

our system of values. We lack the inner unity and vitality necessary to hold together every phase of our civilization. Increasing areas of life, such as business, politics, science, and art have asserted their independence. With few exceptions, they acknowledge no source of authority beyond themselves. This makes for a disorganization rather than for an integration of life.

A civilization that is not integrated will have inner conflicts, confusion, and frustration. A struggle for a reintegration, or at least for a renewal, takes place within the present integrating center. When men lose faith in the ends for which they have lived, they substitute other ends. These ends or values may be unworthy and ultimately self-defeating. This has happened within Western civilization. Values that should be strictly instrumental have become for many people the ends for which they live. Gadgets are considered of more importance than God. Such an inversion of values more or less inevitably results from the decadence of the integrating center of civilization. When that center becomes decadent and hence the civilization disintegrates, new centers tend to develop at the periphery of the civilization. Things that should be secondary and instrumental become primary and ends in themselves; their secondary nature forecasts eventual destruction.

If our analysis is correct, then we can say correctly that if Western civilization collapses, it will be due primarily to inner decay rather than to external pressure. Western civilization will have committed suicide. Also, if this analysis is correct, then the West and the world will not get beyond the present critical period until a new integration takes place. This may be done by adopting the integrating center of a competing civilization or by discovering inner resources for its own renewal. It seems that Western civilization more likely will follow the latter pattern. Why? Primarily because of its relation to and its dependence upon the Christian movement, which contains within itself a remarkable capacity for renewal and survival.

While one should not, and properly cannot, identify Western civilization with the Christian movement, yet the strength of Western civilization has been the ideas and ideals contributed to it primarily by Christianity. This fact is one of the chief sources of hope for the Western world in this crisis.

This implies that the loss of vitality of the integrating center of Western civilization is caused by the decay of organized Christianity itself. This is not a criticism of Christianity as such but of the contemporary organized forms of Christianity. Organized Christianity has lost, to an alarming degree, its power to unify civilization. One reason for that loss—and no doubt the chief reason—is the lack of spiritual power in the churches. For many Christians, and even possibly for most, their religion has been merely a convenience more or less at the circumference of their lives rather than the pulsating dynamic center of their lives. In turn, social groups often fall far below the moral and religious standards of the individuals who compose those groups.

Here is the real heart of the world's problem. The integrating center of Western civilization has become decadent and fails to hold in one closely knit unit all phases of that civilization. This is true because the heart or core of that integrating center has lost so much of its vitality and virility. At the heart or core of the integrating center of civilization, as is true of an individual's system of values, there should be and must be for real strength one supreme value which gives unity and stability to the whole.

The churches are responsible, to a considerable degree, for the decay or lack of vitality of the core of the integrating center of Western civilization. The message they have proclaimed has lost so largely the challenge and dynamic of original Christianity. They have failed to inspire their members to make their love for Christ and their devotion to his cause the central thing in their lives, to which every other phase of their lives has been made subservient.

How do Oriental and other civilizations fit into this whole pattern? We have limited, in the main, our discussion to Western civilization. The suggestion has been made that strong civilizations, such as Western civilization, go through crisis periods primarily because of inner crises rather than because of outer competition. It also has been suggested that a civilization might face a crisis because its integrating center was challenged by the values or the ends of another civilization. This is one reason for the crisis in the Orient.

The peoples of the Orient have been exposed to Western life. So long as they accepted only the means or methods of the West, there was little if any dislocation. These peoples, however, could not adopt the methods or skills of the West without importing some of the ideas of the West. To the degree that they have accepted these ideas or values, their old ideas and values have been challenged. Also, to the degree that the old has been challenged by the new, a crisis has been created at the heart of their civilization. This is one explanation, although admittedly not the only one, of the present confusion in the Orient.

The struggle toward a new integration in the West and of a reorientation of life in the Orient suggests the possibility of the achievement of one unified world civilization. The actual achievement of such a civilization may be in the distant future, but there are some evidences that the world is moving in that direction. There is a possibility that this is one phase of the present world travail.

SECULARIZATION OF LIFE

As suggested previously, as the integrating center of a civilization becomes decadent, new centers evolve. The means of life tend to become the ends for which men live. For example, material things, which should be instrumental and which should be used to promote spiritual ends, have become for millions of people the supreme values in life. This secularization of life, which has reached into every area, is an important element in the contemporary crisis.

What is meant by secularism? It is a system of social ethics based upon a doctrine advanced by G. J. Holyoake (1817–1906) that ethical standards and conduct should be determined exclusively with reference to the present life and social well-being.[2] It is the doctrine that morality should be based solely on the well-being of mankind in the present life to the exclusion of all considerations drawn from belief in God or in a future state.[3] It should be remembered that the term "secular" does not necessarily mean the same thing as "secularism." For example, *The Oxford English Dictionary* defines "secular" as "belonging to the world and its affairs as distinguished from the church and religion; civil, lay, temporal," and suggests that it is used chiefly as a negative term applying to nonreligious or nonsacred things. The school and the state properly may be classified as "secular." This does not mean necessarily that they are secularistic. Their basic philosophy does not have to be secularism.

[2] *Webster's New International Dictionary.*
[3] *The Oxford English Dictionary.*

Spann, considering secularism more as a philosophy, defines it as "an evasive, often unconscious, philosophy which does not deny but ignores the presence and ethical influence of a living God." [4] It is practical atheism, a failure to let God be God in our lives. "Its nature is neither to affirm nor to deny religious faith, but to live indifferently to it." [5]

Secularism may become so predominantly one's philosophy of life that it really becomes the center of his life and hence his religion. This is true of anyone who worships the things of life rather than the God of life.

The spirit of secularism has pervaded all phases of life: literature and art, business and politics, science and education, and even religion itself. The tendency toward complete autonomy in many areas of life is both an evidence of, and in turn a factor in, the increasing secularization of life. If secularism means, as Spann says, the ignoring of the presence and ethical influence of the living God, if it means to live indifferently to religious faith, then much of modern literature, art, science, education, business, and politics would have to be labeled as secularistic in approach and viewpoint. There are exceptions, and there may be some encouraging improvements, but the general picture has been a deepening secularization of these areas of life.

The suggestion has been made that even religion has been affected by the modern spirit of secularism. There is enough truth in the following statement by Davies to make us a little uneasy. He says, "Church members are only a degree less secularized in their consciousness than the public that is completely divorced from the church." [6] This secu-

[4] J. Richard Spann (editor) The Christian Faith and Secularism (New York–Nashville: Abingdon-Cokesbury Press, 1948), p. 5.

[5] Ibid., p. 11.

[6] D. R. Davies, The Sin of Our Age (New York: The Macmillan Co., 1947), p. 61.

larization of church members and of church life is one factor in the loss of vitality of the core or integrating center of our civilization.

The secularized church may have, and usually does have, beautiful and sometimes elaborate church buildings. It may have a properly arranged order of service, with every conceivable aid to worship. It may have, and frequently does have, a highly educated and cultured minister. It even may be reaching great numbers of people in its organizations and services and still largely be a church orientated to this world and not to the Eternal. This is true to the degree that it measures its own success and progress in material rather than in spiritual terms.

It is possible that even the well-meaning efforts of Christian leaders to make every area of life sacred has contributed to the secularization of life. An emphasis on the sacredness of all life may be carried to such an extreme that it will tend to break down proper distinctions between the sacred and the secular. If this happens, it will result in a loss of a sense of the holy and in an indifference to things sacred.

For example, there is a sense in which every day is a holy day. But there is one day that is uniquely holy. This day has been set aside by God himself as a holy day. It is to be a day of rest, a day that is set apart and dedicated to God and to his worship and service in a different way from the other days of the week. Certainly every day for a Christian should be made holy by a sense of the presence of God and by a deep conviction that his workaday task is of God's appointment. He can and should have a sense of divine mission even in a so-called secular vocation. This means that Monday through Saturday can be and should be holy, but the Lord's Day, the day on which Christ arose from the dead, is to be uniquely sacred or holy. Any loss of the sense of the unique holiness of the Lord's Day will tend to break down the sense of the holiness of every other day.

What has been said concerning the Lord's Day could be said concerning the house of God, the tithe, or the call of God to vocational religious service. Every house, such as a shop or a store, the house where one lives, or a government building, can and should become holy because of the presence of God and because the house has been set apart to God and to the fulfilment of his purposes. On the other hand, the church house is uniquely holy. It is dedicated to God, to his worship, and to his service in a different way. It stands in the community as a symbol of God's presence among his people. In like manner, all one has belongs to God, but the tithe is uniquely holy unto him. Likewise, every vocation and profession can and should be used for holy purposes, but the call to minister or to serve as a life's vocation is uniquely holy.

If we should become so secularized as to fail to recognize the uniquely holy or sacred, we would lose sooner or later even the sense of the sacredness or the holiness of the less holy. All of life, even the uniquely holy, would tend to become secularized and, ultimately, our conception of God would bring him down to the level of man. At best he would be a humanized God—hardly more than a reflection of man's limitations.

This is not a plea for an artificial separation between the sacred and the so-called secular and the exaltation of the former. The world has had too much of that in some circles. An example is the sharp distinction that has been made between the clergy on the one hand and the laity on the other. When this distinction is too sharply drawn, it tends not only to handicap the church and the cause but actually contributes to the secularizing of life, at least for the laity.

Whatever may be the factors contributing to the secularization of life, that secularization, particularly of the church, is an evidence of the church's partial failure within history. Instead of overcoming the world, the church has been, to a distressing degree, overcome by the world. "History judges Christianity for having been conquered by history." [7] The Christian movement must free itself from the enslavement of our pagan culture if it is to provide the resources for the renewal and reorientation of our civilization. It must be *in* the world but not of the world.

DETHRONEMENT OF GOD

In discussing the heart of the crisis, we have considered the loss of vitality of the integrating center of civilization and the general secularization of life. We have suggested that these represent different ways of looking at the heart of the trouble. The dethronement or humanizing of God is another approach to the situation.

It also has been said previously that as the center of a civilization becomes weakened or decadent, the civilization itself disintegrates. The more thoroughly the center of a civilization is unified, the more it will permeate and hold together in one unified whole every phase of the civilization. The strength of a civilization can be measured, to a considerable degree, by the depth and thoroughness with which it is permeated by or integrated around a supreme value, or values, which represent the religion of the civilization.

The strength of that center, in turn, depends on how well

[7] Berdyaev, *The Fate of Man in the Modern World*, p. 110.

it is integrated. The most worthy and the most effective center or core for a civilization is devotion to the sovereign God and to his will. What Trueblood says concerning the individual is just as true of a civilization. His statement is as follows: "The only way in which a person may achieve relative unity of life is by dedication to something outside himself. . . . The competing parts of our lives, which cannot unite of themselves, are then united because of a unity of direction, when all parts point one way." [8] Devotion to God and to his will gives that unity of direction. When God is made the center of life, the object of supreme devotion by the individual, the nation, or the civilization, that individual, nation, or civilization will be well integrated and hence will have the internal strength and vitality to meet the challenges of life from within and from without. On the other hand, when God is pushed from the center of life, disintegration, decay, and defeat inevitably follow sooner or later.

There is a similar relation between the secularization of life and the dethronement of God. Life has been largely secularized because God has been dethroned. He is not the supreme object of man's devotion. When God is not central in life, men live as though God does not exist. They do not recognize his authority in their lives. If he is in their lives at all, he is at the circumference. It may be nice to call upon him when it is convenient or when a real emergency arises, but he is not to be permitted to interfere in the everyday affairs of life.

We do not mean by what we have said that Western man or Western civilization has ever put God first in life. We do mean, however, that God has been more central in life than at the present time. Increasing areas of life have

[8] *The Life We Prize*, p. 52.

asserted their independence of God's authority. This self-asserting independence in so many realms of life is a major cause of the disintegration of modern civilization.

Among the chief forces that shape a culture or a civilization are the spiritual presuppositions of a religious or ethical nature which Emil Brunner calls "the culture-transcendent presuppositions of every culture." [9] One of those culture-transcendent presuppositions of Christianity is the existence of a holy, righteous, sovereign God who claims for himself authority over the affairs of men, and whose will is the final determinant of right and wrong for men. A secularized culture has no place for such a concept or presupposition.

Western man has usurped the place that properly belongs to God. He has dethroned God and put himself on the throne. Some students of world affairs consider this the major sin of our age and the chief contributor to the ills of our day.[10] Paradoxically, when man exalts himself, he ultimately debases himself. In other words, the statement of Jesus that he who would exalt himself will be debased is in harmony with human experience.

When man dethrones God and exalts himself to the place that properly belongs to God, he separates himself from God. He no longer recognizes his subserviency to, and his dependence upon, God. When he thus separates himself from God, he separates himself from the source of his own dignity and worth. Man was made in the image of God. He was made for fellowship with God. When he egotistically exalts himself to the place that belongs to God, he finds that ultimately he lowers himself to the mere ani-

[9] *Christianity and Civilization* (New York: Charles Scribner's Sons, 1948), Part I, p. 11.
[10] See particularly Davies, *The Sin of Our Age.*

mal level. The only thing that makes man different from the animals of the field is his kinship and fellowship with God. There have been abundant demonstrations in recent years of the ultimate results of a divorcement of man from God. One result is the terrible inhumanity of man to man as revealed in the internment camps of the Nazis and the prison camps of the Communists.

Nicholas Berdyaev, in his graphic style, summarizes this whole idea as follows:

To affirm himself and preserve the source of his creative energy, man must affirm God as well. He must affirm the image of God within him. For he can have no vision of himself if he has none of the higher Divine nature. . . . The affirmation of the human individuality and personality demands a tie with a higher Divine principle. But when the human personality will admit no authority but itself, it disintegrates, allowing the intrusion of the lowest natural elements which consume it. When man will admit only himself, he loses consciousness of himself.[11]

As Berdyaev suggests, one reason why Western civilization has exhausted, to such a great extent, its creativity is the fact that it has divorced itself from God, who is the source of man's creative ability.

A major contributor to the dethronement or the humanizing of God has been humanism. Humanism, as it was revived in the days of the Renaissance, was largely theistic. Although there has continued to be a theistic element in some humanism, yet the general trend has been increasingly anthropocentric. Man has been so exalted that God has been pushed aside. In recent years, the world has been reaping some of the inevitable results of such a nontheistic humanism.

11 *The Meaning of History*, pp. 154–5.

Humanism even has infiltrated theological ranks. Much liberal theology, at least of a generation ago, was largely humanistic. Man was made central, with God given a secondary status. In theology, as in other areas, there has been in recent years some reaction to this humanistic emphasis. This is one explanation for the rise and influence of Neo-Protestantism.

We do not mean that humanism was, and is, all bad. The movement has made important and distinctive contributions to the world. The ultimate results, however, of a humanism divorced from God are tragic for man and civilization. Even in a theistic humanism there is the constant danger of exalting man to the place that belongs to God.

Closely akin to man's exaltation of himself was his blind faith that all he needed to solve his problems and the problems of his world were more knowledge, more power, and more freedom. We are beginning to see, however, that what the world needs is not more knowledge, unless it is the knowledge of God; not more power, unless it is the power that comes from the Eternal; and not more freedom, unless it is the freedom that comes from knowing the Truth.

The primary trouble with our world is lack of devotion to the living God—a God whom the world has elbowed out of his rightful place of centrality. Having pushed God out of the center of life, the world has little place for the otherworldly or the eternal. It finds its point of reference within the time process. Its main values are material and temporal. They are in the here and now. The arbitrator of values is within man himself rather than within the will of a sovereign, transcendent God. However, when man thus dethrones God, who is the true spiritual center of his being, he creates false centers at the periphery of his life and initiates a process by which he weakens or devitalizes his own personality.

Thus we see that the dethronement of God by the modern world has created problems within man and within his world. This dethronement is at the very heart of the crisis within man and within Western civilization. The tragic thing is that God is not as central as he should be, even in many churches and religious groups. This means that our churches cannot provide the leadership that the world needs until they repent and come to a deepened devotion to the eternal God and to his will for them and for the world.

LOSS OF FAITH

Many students of Western civilization are in agreement concerning the basic ills of our civilization, although they may express their common convictions in different terms. Most of them agree that Western civilization is desperately sick and that this sickness has resulted from a loss of its faith. They would agree with the following statement that was made by Harold J. Laski during World War II: "The most important war aim that is before us is the recovery of the faith by which we can all of us stand." [12] This recovery of faith is crucially important because "human societies, like human beings, live by faith and die when faith dies." [13]

As suggested previously, Western man has lost his faith in the basic moral principles and fundamental spiritual ideals or theological concepts that have provided much of

[12] *Faith, Reason, and Civilization*, p. 33.
[13] Whittaker Chambers, "I Was the Witness," *Saturday Evening Post*, February 9, 1952, p. 18.

the foundation for Western civilization. What John Macmurray says primarily of England and Europe could be said of the West in general. He says that he cannot think of anything that we used to believe in that we still believe in passionately and with our whole hearts. He further adds: "Our ideals seem to have gone dead; we no longer believe in them; and we don't disbelieve in them either. That is our dilemma. We neither believe nor disbelieve. We are neither hot nor cold; and it paralyzes our capacity to decide and to act." [14]

The West, in the main, has lost its faith and has not discovered a new faith to take its place. It must be admitted, of course, that this loss of faith is not complete and that it has gone further in Europe, as has the general disintegration, than in the United States. But who would dare to say that it has not gone far enough in the United States to threaten the foundations of our American way of life?

This loss of faith is an important element in the weakening of the integrating center of Western civilization. Unless there is a strong, virile faith at the center of life, that center cannot influence all of life and thus mold all phases of life into a well-integrated whole. This is just as true of a nation or a civilization as it is of an individual.

In addition to the loss of faith in the basic principles that have provided much of the strength and internal unity of Western civilization, there are other phases of this loss of faith, and some of these are of considerable importance.

For example, Western man has lost much of his faith in science. There was a time when the peoples of the more advanced nations considered science as the savior of mankind. They believed that science was in the process of giv-

[14] *Freedom in the Modern World* (second edition; London: Faber & Faber Ltd., 1935), p. 28.

ing to man the resources by which he could understand and solve all his problems and the problems of his world. Science was contributing so much to the lifting of the burdens of the world and to the general enrichment of life that, ultimately, the general level of life would be so raised that men would have a veritable heaven on earth.

We are not attempting here to belittle or to deprecate the contributions of science. It is marvelous what science has contributed to our world. Men were never justified, however, in placing so much faith in science. One reason they went down that dead-end street was the fact that they measured life in temporal or material terms. They failed to realize that science could make men more powerful but that it could not make them better. Some branches of science could give a better understanding of man, but they were powerless to change the inner nature and motives of man.

In the contemporary period man has been rather rudely awakened to the limitations of science. He has realized rather suddenly that science is impartial, that it does not and cannot decide the purposes for which it will be used. It may be used to enrich or to impoverish, to free or to enslave, to strengthen or to destroy, to bring life or death. Man decides the purposes for which science will be used. A great preacher expressed the idea when he said, "I am not afraid of the atom bomb; I am afraid of the hand that controls the bomb." And we should remember that science does not and cannot control the hand that controls what science has placed in that hand. This realization of the limitations and even the possible destructiveness of science has been a rather rude shock to Western man, who had tended to worship at the throne of science.

One encouraging element in the contemporary scene is

the fact that many scientists, particularly outstanding ones, have been among the first to admit the limitations and even the dangers of science. It is possible that the most scared and the most humble people in the world today are the atomic scientists, who know the potentialities of what they have given to the world. They are fearful of what their own discoveries may do for the world.

Closely akin to man's loss of faith in science has been his loss of faith in the inevitable progress of history. This has been the predominant view or philosophy of history of modern man as contrasted to the classical view and the biblical or Christian view.[15] Emil Brunner says that this idea of idealistic progressivism was "the bastard off-spring of an optimistic anthropology and Christian eschatology."[16] The "optimistic anthropology" was largely the product of humanism. The contribution of Christian eschatology was through the Christian concept of a kingdom of God, which ultimately would be triumphant, and through the Christian's expectation of the return of the Lord.

Regardless of the source of the idea of inevitable progress, it became the working faith, "the animating and controlling idea of western civilization."[17] This idea has evoked "all the enthusiasm and faith of a genuine religion."[18] It created for man what many have called "The Century of Hope."

Nineteenth-century man, in the main, was possessed and almost obsessed with the social interpretation of the king-

[15] See Reinhold Niebuhr, *Faith and History* (New York: Charles Scribner's Sons, 1949), for a discussion of the various theories or philosophies of history.

[16] *Op. cit.*, p. 55.

[17] J. B. Bury, *The Idea of Progress* (London: Macmillan and Co. Ltd., 1920), p. vii.

[18] Christopher H. Dawson, *Progress and Religion* (New York: Longmans, Green & Co., 1929), p. 201.

dom of God. This kingdom was to be realized on this earth and largely through man's efforts. Man had a blind faith that the processes of history were in themselves redemptive. He believed that with a little more power, a little more knowledge, a little more freedom, and a little more time, man could make the world into the beloved community. The power, knowledge, and freedom would come as the benefits of science, education, and democracy were extended in the world.

Men have come to see, however, what some few men saw all the time, that such a blind faith in history and in the historic process was, and is, ill-founded. It was a tragic mistake to identify the kingdom of God with any stage of past, present, or future history unless the latter would include divine, eternal history. It was likewise a mistake to identify the processes of history with the will of God.

While God is active in the world, and his will ultimately will be done in the world, that is quite different from saying that the world inevitably will progress. This is particularly true if we measure progress in human terms. While we may believe that God's kingdom is an active, dynamic, present reality in the world, yet it is a mistake to identify it with any earthly program or achievement. It is infinitely broader and bigger than any or all man-made and man-led programs. It is a spiritual kingdom and cannot be contained in human or earthly forms.

We say this primarily to point out that man should never have placed his faith in the inevitable progress of history. Such a faith is justified only when history is within the will of God and is under the control of the hand of God. We already have suggested that history is never so completely under the control of God that it properly can be identified with his will.

Whatever may have been the factors in the disillusionment of men, it is certainly true that what was a century of hope has changed into a century of despair. "Faith in the boundless possibilities of progress which was the inspiration of the nineteenth century is almost at vanishing point." [19] Reinhold Niebuhr says, "Since 1914 one tragic experience has followed another, as if history had been designed to refute the vain delusions of modern man." [20] He further suggests that "the tragic irony of this refutation by contemporary history of modern man's conception of history embodies the spiritual crisis of our age." [21] The contradiction between the hopes of yesterday and the grim realities of today has created in some sections of the world something like despair and "is generating a kind of desperate complacency in those parts of the world in which the crisis of the age is dimly, though not fully, sensed." [22] One area gripped by this "desperate complacency" is the United States.

Another phase of man's general disillusionment is his loss of faith in himself. He is not nearly so optimistic as he formerly was concerning human nature and man's ability to solve his problems. He is in the process of understanding that it will require more than more knowledge, more power, more freedom, and more time to solve his problems. He is even coming to see that these things may actually deepen his problems and create new ones for him.

One factor in man's loss of faith in himself is his deepened insight into the problems of his world. He now sees that these problems are much more serious than he had once thought. He now understands that there are forces at work in the world that are beyond his ability to control.

[19] Berdyaev, *Towards a New Epoch*, p. v.
[20] *Op. cit.*, pp. 6–7.
[21] *Ibid.*, p. 8.
[22] *Ibid.*, p. 13.

Too frequently, however, he merely sits down and folds his hands with a sense of frustration or a feeling of complacent futility.

Possibly the most tragic phase of man's loss of faith has been the fact that at the very time when he needs most a strong, undergirding faith in God, he does not have enough faith in God to sustain him. We are not saying that this loss of faith is universal. Thousands, possibly even millions, of Christian men and women have retained a strong, abiding sense of the presence of the living God and hence a triumphant faith in him. These individuals have the inner resources to face the problems of life courageously and to possess an inner peace that passeth understanding.

Generally speaking, however, Western man has lost his faith in God, and lost it at the time when he needs it most. Many things have contributed to this loss of faith, but man's unrealistic faith in science, in the inevitable progress of history, and in his ability to solve his problems and the problems of the world was, and is, a major factor in his loss of faith in God. In other words, when man thinks he does not need God, he tends to push him aside. He seems to think, at such a time, that recognition of his dependence on God would be a sign of weakness. As a result, when man becomes conscious of his need for God, he finds that God is not readily available.

The ultimate result of man's loss of faith in science, in history, in himself, and in God will depend on what he does about his loss of faith or what he lets his loss of faith do for, and to, him.

His loss of faith may be a curse or a blessing. It will be a curse to him if it leaves him permanently in a state of despair and futility. It will be a curse to him if he turns to the group or collective to recover his sense of importance and security. If he recaptures his faith in himself and in the historic process by identifying himself and his interests with the group, he will tend to have less of a sense of need for God and of God's place and function in the world. The collective may fulfil, from his viewpoint, the functions of God, and hence it may become his god.

There are indications that many men are turning to the collective. The rapid progress of communism in the world cannot be understood apart from man's loss of faith in himself and in his search for some basis for the renewal of his faith. This groping for a faith to live by has been one reason for the rise of every mass movement of the contemporary period. Modern man needs to know, however, that if he places his faith in the collective, he will discover ultimately that his faith has been misplaced. The collective cannot satisfy the deeper needs of man. He also will discover, sooner or later, that, instead of finding himself by identifying himself with the group, he will lose himself. The collective will enslave and depersonalize him. He will not recapture his faith in himself. He will be gripped by a deepening despair.

It should be understood that we have not attempted to evaluate in general collectivism or to appraise specific collectivistic movements. We have considered only the relation of the collective to man's search for a living faith—a faith that will help him to recapture the sense of his own significance and a reasonable faith in life itself. We simply have suggested that the collective will not and cannot meet man's need for such a faith.

On the other hand, it is possible that man's loss of faith in science, in the inevitable progress of history, and even in himself may be a blessing to him. This *may* be true if it causes him to recognize that he needs a power outside himself to solve his problems and the problems of his world; it *will* be true only if he turns to God as that power. A return to God will enable man to see that any permanent progress is impossible unless he progresses in his understanding of God and of God's way with, and his will for, man. Man in fellowship with God will see that even he himself can have no real significance apart from God.

If man learns the difficult lesson of his limitations and of God's limitless power, then the present period of defeat and despair will be a blessing to him and to his world. Time alone will reveal whether or not man is going to be intelligent enough and spiritually alert enough to learn this lesson. "We have got to get back to God. Unless the world gets back to God, it hasn't a chance. We ought to hurry back to God." [23]

[23] J. A. Spender, in Major, *op. cit.*, p. 9.

6

CURE FOR THE CRISIS

LET us turn now from a diagnosis of the crisis in the preceding chapters to some suggestions concerning the cure for the crisis. Civilization, particularly Western civilization, is desperately sick. Sometimes when the cause, or causes, of a disease are discovered, the remedy is comparatively simple, while on other occasions it requires drastic and speedy action. It now seems that the illness of contemporary civilization will require the latter.

We should remember that outer symptoms are frequently misleading. The wise doctor does not treat the symptoms. Rather, he uses them to help him to diagnose the real source, or sources, of the trouble. They may be merely the figment of the imagination of the patient or they may be symptoms that are common to entirely different diseases. Many who seek to prescribe for our sick civilization deal exclusively with symptoms. There is no cure in such a procedure.

Certainly this book is not intended as an exhaustive diagnosis of the sickness of our civilization. We have emphasized that any phenomenon of the proportions of the present crisis is very complex. It is possible that some important phases of the present crisis have not been touched on at all, while others have been discussed inadequately. An attempt has been made, however, to outline the major sources of, and factors in, the crisis, but at the same time to suggest that all of these are so closely interrelated that we can speak properly of one basic cause or reason for it.

PRELIMINARY QUESTIONS

Before we consider the suggested cure or remedy for the present crisis, we might raise the prior question, Is there any hope for our civilization? Some men such as Spengler would answer no. They contend that the death of a civilization is just as inevitable as the death of an individual. Cultures and civilizations go through the same life cycle as individuals. Western civilization has reached its senility.

On the other hand, some men hold on desperately to the theory of the inevitable progress of history. Regression periods may occur, but they contend that civilization inevitably marches on. The present may be a critical period for civilization, but it is merely the introductory phase of a richer and higher type of civilization.

Some of the most acute diagnosticians of the contemporary crisis who no longer hold to the inevitable progress theory are, nevertheless, rather optimistic concerning its outcome. For example, Sorokin suggests that, following the decay and collapse of our sensate culture, an ideational type of culture will arise to take its place. He bases his faith largely on the history of similar transition periods in civilizations of the past.[1] Berdyaev reveals a somewhat similar faith, although he does not use the same terminology as

[1] *The Crisis of Our Age*, p. 13.

Sorokin. According to him, there is a rhythm in history as there is in nature, and we are standing at the beginning of a new Middle Ages. The Middle Ages was a period of cultural integration.[2] This concept is quite similar to Sorokin's idea of an ideational civilization—a civilization that is unified around one dominant idea such as God.

It is possible that the birth of a new world is inevitable, but a new world cannot be born without travail. Every major transition period is accompanied by chaos and confusion, by struggle and wars. As Berdyaev expresses it, "in the process of its reincarnation the world must apparently go through a period of darkness."[3] Berdyaev, however, reminds us: "Night is not less wonderful than day, it is equally the work of God; it is lit by the splendour of the stars and it reveals to us things that the day does not know. Night is closer than the day to the mystery of all beginning."[4] Civilizations as well as individuals may learn through suffering, and such learning "may be the sovereign means of progress."[5]

Now what is our answer to the question, Is there a cure for the contemporary crisis? There is no cure or remedy if we are thinking in terms of the restoration of what we have had, of the saving of civilization as it is. "*Western civilization does not deserve to be preserved as it is, and every effort to preserve it as it is will produce its own opposite, by a kind of moral necessity.*"[6] Civilization, particularly Western civilization, needs to be saved, and can be saved if it wants to be saved and wants to be saved badly enough.

While there is a cure for the ills of civilization, yet we

[2] *The End of Our Time*, p. 69.
[3] *Towards a New Epoch*, p. vi.
[4] *The End of Our Time*, pp. 70–71.
[5] Toynbee, *Civilization on Trial*, p. 15.
[6] Horton, *op. cit.*, p. 5.

should remember that, just as the illness is not superficial, so the remedy must not deal with superficial symptoms. Drastic steps must be taken if civilization is to be saved, if the transition period is to be shortened, and if the suffering that accompanies such a period is to be reduced.

Another question is, Is there one cure or more than one cure for the sickness of civilization? In other words, is the title of this chapter correct, or is it an oversimplification?

Although we have stressed that the crisis is a complicated phenomenon and that it is so serious that every phase of life is, and will be, affected by it, nevertheless, we have suggested that it stems from one basic cause. This basic cause we labeled in the last chapter as the heart of the crisis and suggested that there might be, and are, different ways of looking at that heart or basic cause.

Throughout the diagnosis of the crisis, we have attempted to point out that every phase of it has a spiritual base. We suggested that this is just as true of the economic and political phases of the crisis as of the more strictly religious. One reason for this is the fact that when the spiritual is properly understood and interpreted, it is as broad as life itself. Every area of life is to be included within the interest, and ultimately within the domain, of spiritual religion. Any tendency to compartmentize life and restrict religion to one segment or phase of it contributes to the disintegration and disorganization of life.

Just as there is a chief cause of the crisis, which may be examined from several viewpoints, in like manner there is a cure for the crisis that may be studied from several standpoints. However, in the broadest and most accurate sense, it is *one* cure rather than several cures.

We do not say this to belittle the contributions that may be made to the solution of our problems by social scientists, practical politicians, and others. Christian forces and leaders should recognize their need for the co-operation of all men of good will. The Christian ideal and program must be implemented to become socially effective. On the other hand, social scientists and politicians will not make their most effective contribution to the solution of the problems of the world if they restrict themselves to tinkering with the machinery or to treating symptoms. The real disease in every area is basically moral and spiritual, and a spiritual remedy alone will remove the conditions that have brought on the disease.

One other preliminary question that possibly should be asked is, Is a cure inevitable? Assuming that a cure is possible, is it inevitable that the world will come through successfully the present transition period? Some ask, Does not history teach us that civilization muddles through some way and eventually discovers a way out of every crisis?

The answer to the last question is definitely no. There are more dead civilizations than live ones.[7] It is true that some civilizations that have died have furnished the seeds for a new civilization. The latter is what Toynbee calls an affiliated civilization—one that is affiliated or related to a former civilization.[8]

Throughout this discussion we have expressed a rather optimistic view concerning the inner renewal and hence the survival of Western civilization. But we would be out of harmony with the history of civilizations if we suggested that such a survival was inevitable. Western civilization

[7] Arnold Toynbee, in *A Study of History*, one volume edition (New York: Oxford University Press, 1946), p. 244, says that sixteen of twenty-six known civilizations are now dead, that two others are in their last agonies, and that seven of the remaining are under threat of either annihilation or assimilation by the eighth, which is Western civilization.

[8] *Ibid.*, p. 77.

must meet certain conditions if it is to survive. It remains to be seen whether or not Western man is going to meet those conditions quickly enough to save himself.

As we have said and shall say more specifically later, the chief hope for the renewal and the survival of Western civilization is the Christian religion. While Christianity cannot and should not be identified with that civilization, it has contributed a great deal to the West, and particularly to what has been its integrating center. The Christian movement has demonstrated over and over again a most remarkable capacity for survival.

The close relationship of Western civilization with the Christian movement—that is, the organized forms of Christianity—does not mean, however, the inevitable survival of Western civilization. There is a great difference between Christianity as such and its organized forms; and even though the Christian movement should survive, the civilization which was the channel for the expression of that movement would not necessarily survive. Whether Western civilization lives or dies will depend not only on what that civilization does, but also on what happens within the Christian movement itself. *Christianity* will not fail, but the organized forms of Christianity have, at times, failed, and may fail again and be replaced by organized forms that will be better adapted to meet the deeper needs of the contemporary world.

Now, what is the cure for the crisis and the conditions that must be met if civilization is to be saved?

RETURN TO GOD

Whatever approach we may make to the problems of our day, we discover that man's departure from God is a definite factor in the crisis we face. If we think of the crux of the crisis as the disintegration of the integrating center of civilization, we discover, as previously suggested, that that disintegration came as a result of man's departure from God, who is the only object worthy of the supreme devotion of the individual or of a civilization. If man is to discover the resources for the renewal of the integrating center of his civilization, he must return to God. God must be made central, not only in his individual life, but also in the life of his world.

We should remember, however, that the results of a return to God will be determined by the God to whom men return. Only a return to the God revealed in the life and teachings of Jesus will lead men to repent of their sins and to find the renewal they need. A return to such a God will give the world the vital type of religion that is essential if the heart of civilization is to be reintegrated and revived. If that heart is not revived, there will be no hope for civilization.

The first necessary step, if man and his civilization are to return to the God revealed by Jesus, is a spirit of genuine repentance. It may sound paradoxical, but repentance is man's first step in his return to God; and, on the other hand, a consciousness of the presence of God deepens the sense of sin and of a need for repentance. The first reaction of any man who has had a vision of the Lord high and lifted up is the reaction of Isaiah, who cried out: "Woe is me! for I am undone; because I am a man of unclean lips, and I dwell in the midst of a people of unclean lips: for mine eyes have seen the King, Jehovah of hosts." [9] When men become conscious of the presence of God, they realize that "all have sinned, and come short of the glory of God,"

[9] Isa. 6:5 ASV.

that "there is none righteous, no, not one." This is true not only of all men, but also of all nations and civilizations.

A sense of sin attended by a genuine spirit of repentance by the peoples of the nations of the world would go a long ways toward solving the problems of our world. What Davies says concerning Europe could be said about all other sections of the world: "Repentance, not just intelligence, is Europe's vital need to-day. The current assumption that what the world chiefly suffers from is stupidity is utterly inadequate and shallow." [10] The same author also says, "*Western civilization must repent its titantic, basic sin.*" [11] For Davies, the basic sin is man's exaltation of himself to the place that properly belongs to God, and to God alone. For this spirit of repentance to be adequate, it cannot be restricted to isolated individuals; it must become general enough that nations and even civilizations will repent. The glorious thing is that our God is always ready to forgive if we will only repent. The prophet Amos proclaimed a message to Israel that our nation and our civilization need. He repeated the challenging and yet reassuring words, "Seek Jehovah, and ye shall live." [12]

A proper sense of God's presence also will give to man a keener insight into the depth and seriousness of sin in his own life and also in the social order. It will enable him to recognize his limitations in the battle against sin and will lead him to admit frankly and unashamedly his dependence upon God. It will keep him from identifying the kingdom of God with any social program or political or ecclesiastical organization. He will recognize that sin is a positive factor in every human institution or social program, and that this

[10] D. R. Davies, *The Sin of Our Age*, p. 6.
[11] *Ibid.*, p. 123.
[12] Amos 5:6 ASV; cf. 5:4, 14.

is true both of the status quo and of programs of change. In this way he will be saved from some of the errors of the visionary idealist. Likewise, a sense of the sinfulness of sin and of its presence, even in the best of programs, will help to save man from placing his faith in the work of the "prophets of the half-way house." [13] The situation is too serious for halfway measures.

Some students of world affairs contend that there is no solution for the problems of the world, and particularly no hope for an effective, political reorganization of the world, unless there can be developed a sense of world community or unity. This emphasis is particularly prominent in one of Daniel J. Fleming's books. He says: "Enlarging our circle of consciousness to include a world fraternity involves an unprecedented mental and spiritual change within us . . . love of mankind is little more than an ideal which now presses for embodiment." [14]

What is our hope of attaining such a world community, of enlarging the circle of our consciousness to include a world fraternity, of achieving this necessary but unprecedented change? There is only one justifiable hope, and that is in God. Maritain suggests that "man without God cannot find unity except against another," [15] and he is not talking about the unity of the individual. It should be added that unity attained by any social group—national, racial, or otherwise—uniting against another group will result ultimately in disunity and will be self-defeating. The only unity or community that will last is a unity achieved in the spirit of love. Such a spirit results only from a sense of fel-

[13] D. R. Davies, *op. cit.*, p. 124.
[14] Daniel J. Fleming, *Bringing Our World Together* (New York: Charles Scribner's Sons, 1945), p. vii. The subtitle of the book is *A Study in World Community*.
[15] *The Twilight of Civilization*, p. 38.

lowship with a God who is love; one whom those who know call "our Father." Fleming says the task of world community is so tremendous "that our faith in a successful outcome might well fail us, were it not for the conviction that God wills it." [16] He might have added that what God wills he ultimately achieves.

The spirit of world community cannot become a living reality except as men co-operate with God in manifesting his spirit and in doing his will in the world. Even in this co-operative work man is dependent upon God. Only as man is conscious of the presence of God and has a sense of a vital partnership with God can he have the dynamic drive to press constantly toward the attainment of God's will in his own life and in the world. The most irresistible force in the world except God is a man who has an abiding sense of a divine mission. Difficulties may challenge him, but they will not and cannot defeat him. He has a conviction that he is laboring together with a sovereign, undefeatable God.

Man must return to God if he is to recover or to renew his creative abilities. Nothing can so heighten man's powers and so stimulate every phase of his personality as an awareness of the presence of the living God. What is true for the individual is true for a civilization. Western civilization has strayed away from God and hence has divorced itself from the springs of its own creativity. To recover, it must return to God, who is the source of light and life.

Let us repeat what we have emphasized previously: We are not going to solve the problems of our world unless the peoples of the world come to God in humble repentance of their sins and enthrone him at the center of their lives. "God must again be the centre of our whole life—our

[16] Op. cit., p. viii.

thought, our feeling, our only dream, our only desire, our only hope." [17]

This return to God must begin with individual men and women, but it must not stop there if it is to save civilization. God must be placed at the center of all of life. Business and the professions, science and philosophy must bow down before God and recognize their dependence upon him and dedicate themselves to the fulfilment of his will among men. Only through such a thorough return unto God can God become the center of our civilization. We must stop trying to serve two masters.

It is recognized that this is an idealistic program; also, that its fulfilment will not be attained completely. This much, however, can be said: To the degree that the world makes God central in its life, and to that degree only, will the basic problems of our world be solved and health and vitality return to our body politic.

It may sound paradoxical, but if man loses his faith in his ability to solve his problems and the problems of his world and turns to God for needed guidance and strength, he will find that such a turning to God will renew his faith not only in God, but also in his ability, with the help of God, to make a significant contribution to the solution of the problems of his world. In other words, man, by losing faith in himself and placing his faith in God, recaptures his faith in himself.

The same thing can be said about man's loss of faith in the historic process. When man recaptures his faith in a sovereign God, he can and will recover his faith in history. The difference is that now his faith is centered in divine history rather than in strictly human history.

By this we do not mean a return to a blind faith in the

[17] Berdyaev, *The End of Our Time*, p. 106.

redemptive nature of the historic process. It does mean, however, a strong abiding faith in God's redemptive purposes in history; a faith that history is under the guiding hand of a sovereign God. The latter does not mean that the kingdom of God can or will be realized fully within human history; it does mean that the kingdom of God will be triumphant over history and triumphant within history. As children of God we can be assured that we are serving a God who will be victorious in the world. That assurance will be proportionate to our concept of God.

When we come to realize that God is the only hope of the world, we shall discover that the Christian's faith in God has a unique relevance for times of darkness and despair. "Christian faith is at home . . . with human tragedy, disaster, suffering and frustration." [18] Sometimes men see more clearly in the dark. If the present darkness causes men to turn to the "true light, even the light which lighteth every man, coming into the world," [19] it will be a blessing to man and to his world.

At least Christians should not be too discouraged by the darkness around them. They should remember that the God to whom they belong has not vacated. He is still on his throne. The time will come when "the kingdom of the world is become the kingdom of our Lord, and of his Christ: and he shall reign for ever and ever." [20] Sooner or later every knee shall bow and every tongue shall "confess that Jesus Christ is Lord, to the glory of God the Father." [21] Such assurance should give us a deep, abiding calm and a peace that passeth understanding, even in the midst of the storms that are breaking around us.

[18] Davies, op. cit., p. 135.
[19] John 1:9 ASV.
[20] Rev. 11:15 ASV.
[21] Phil. 2:10–11; cf. Rom. 14:11.

RENEWAL OF ORGANIZED CHRISTIANITY

The diseased condition of our civilization is so serious and the Christian movement is related so closely to Western civilization that a re-examination of the Christian movement itself seems advisable. Organized Christianity, at any particular period, inevitably will be influenced by its environment. It tends, more or less, to become a part of the social order, frequently becoming a defender of the status quo and the most conservative force in society. At times it becomes so involved in the world and the affairs of the world that it no longer challenges the world—like salt that has lost its savor.

Thus a return to God does not mean necessarily the same thing as a return to the church or the churches. The churches themselves may need to return to God. At least they should repent for their share in the sins of the world. Such repentance will enable them to rediscover the sources for their own spiritual renewal.

The Christian movement has demonstrated, over and over again, that it not only can survive the crisis periods when new cultures and civilizations have arisen, but, when renewed, it can be the instrument of God in reviving an existing civilization or in providing an integrating center for a new civilization. "Christianity has arrested cultural decay and saved the essential values of civilization more than once, in the history of the West. Even when it appeared to have become an inert factor in Western history, it has exhibited the power to renew its active influence through self-criticism and reform. Why not again?" [22] It should encourage us that Christianity in its organized

[22] Horton, *op. cit.*, p. 63.

forms "is going through a crisis and longs for some kind of renewal or renaissance." [23]

Contemporary organized Christianity seems to be powerless to save civilization. What are the sources of its weakness? The weakness of contemporary Christianity is not lack of numbers, financial support, or educated leadership. In the United States at least there are more church members with a higher cultural and educational level than ever before. Increasing numbers of college and seminary trained men and women occupy places of leadership in our churches and denominations. Although we are still giving proportionately little to the cause of Christ, more money is being raised for church and religious purposes than ever before. We must look elsewhere for the real weakness of contemporary Christianity.

An evangelism that stresses quantity rather than quality, a stewardship that centers on material rather than on human and spiritual values, and an emphasis on leadership that magnifies primarily better education and training rather than genuine character and spirituality, will not touch the deeper problems of modern organized Christianity. We need more Christians, but far more we need better Christians. We need more adequate financial support, but far more we need increasing numbers of Christians who will recognize that they belong to God, that they are his stewards. We need a better-trained leadership, but even more we need a more consecrated and devoted leadership.

We should remember also that while the many divisions of the Christian group, particularly within Protestantism, may be unfortunate, these divisions are not the main source of our weakness. They are more symptomatic of our weakness than the weakness itself. Possibly Protestantism should

[23] Berdyaev, *Towards a New Epoch*, p. 49.

have fewer sects and denominations, but it is in greater need of more Christian individuals and groups who have deep convictions and a sense of divine mission. Any attempt toward an artificial, external union of groups will not get to the root of the deeper problems of modern Christianity and of contemporary civilization, but actually may deepen those problems.

One thing that is wrong with the present forms of Christianity is what Trueblood calls a sort of vague or mild religiosity. He says, "We are equally shocked at hearing the faith rejected and seeing it practiced." [24] Such a mild sort of religion cannot support a sagging civilization and "cannot long maintain itself." [25]

If Christianity is to perform its functions in the individual and in the world, it cannot be one of several compartments of life. When life is so compartmentized, Christianity and Christian principles are usually pushed out to the circumference of life. It is natural, however, for individuals and civilizations to seek a basis of integration. Supreme value will be attached to something or to some things. Such a supreme value becomes the religion of the individual or civilization. If the Christian religion is pushed to the periphery of life, then false religious centers tend to become the integrating center of life. Such false religions can never meet the deeper needs of their adherents—individuals, nations, or civilizations.

Organized Christianity has been too ready to accept her existing status as merely one phase, and frequently a secondary phase, of life. In the main, it has become so secularized that it has adjusted itself to the compartmental idea. Berdyaev sums up the situation as follows: "Modern Chris-

[24] *Foundations of Reconstruction*, p. 38.
[25] *Ibid.*, p. 39.

tianity is degenerating because it has been relegated to a corner of the human soul and has ceased to be a totalitarian attitude toward life, as, of course, it should be." [26] Modern totalitarian regimes have arisen largely as a result of Christianity's failure to be spiritually totalitarian. Man demands some center around which he can build his life. He needs and wants some cause bigger than himself for which he will be willing to die. Christianity can and should be that cause, but it will be only if it demands the supreme love and loyalty of men. It must recapture the spirit of martyrdom which has characterized the Christian movement in its periods of greatest vitality and triumph.

The Christian movement also needs to recover a deep sense of mission or at least to reinterpret and re-emphasize its mission. Its first and most basic purpose is to deliver its message of salvation to all men. This phase of the Christian program is not only important because of what it means to individuals, but also because of what those individuals will mean to society. There is no social reconstruction without the redemption of individuals.

The Christian mission is not restricted to the individual, but it is all-inclusive. This all-inclusiveness needs to be reinterpreted and re-emphasized. Christianity's mission is worldwide. The continuing commission of Jesus is: "Go ye therefore, and make disciples of all the nations, baptizing them into the name of the Father and of the Son and of the Holy Spirit: teaching them to observe all things whatsoever I commanded you: and lo, I am with you always, even unto the end of the world." [27] A casual knowledge of the commands of Jesus will convince one that the disciple of Jesus is to apply the Christian spirit to every phase of his

[26] *Towards a New Epoch*, p. 106.
[27] Matt. 28:19–20 ASV.

life. The Christian movement must declare the full gospel to all the people of all the world, helping those reached to understand that this message is to be applied to all areas of their lives.

In carrying out this inclusive mission, the Christian churches should not neglect the marching masses who are such an important factor in the contemporary crisis. Many of these masses are in our local communities, but millions of them are also out at the far corners of the earth. It is time for the Christian churches to get dead serious about carrying the gospel to the peoples of the world. They need to lift up their eyes and look on the fields that are white unto harvest. We had better remember that it may be later than we think. The times demand more than ordinary efforts. The next few years may determine the destiny of our nation, our civilization, and our world.

It is not organized Christianity's business to attempt to save our nation or our civilization as such. Christianity's forces should not give divine approval to any particular order or system. The Christian movement should serve as the independent moral and spiritual critic of the world. While churches should not stand in judgment against the cultures and civilizations of the world, yet they should, by proclaiming the gospel message, make the Christian movement the moral conscience of civilization. It should be the voice of the prophet pronouncing judgment upon the world but in the same breath delivering a message of hope and redemption to individuals, to nations, and to civilizations. This prophetic element, which has characterized Christianity at its best, needs to be recaptured.

Although the Christian movement performs very imperfectly its God-given functions in the modern world, nevertheless, there is hope for its renewal and hence for a better performance of its functions. The Christian movement has within "creative forces that are eternally young." [28] There lives "in the depths of Christianity . . . an inexhaustible spiritual power and the possibility of re-birth." [29] Christianity contains a prophetic element with the power of self-criticism, an element that keeps its face toward the future.

What are some of the essential steps or phases in the renewal of contemporary Christianity? The first step is genuine repentance within the Christian movement itself. Organized Christianity is involved in the present crisis, and its own inner dislocation and disintegration are contributors to it. It is no time for a holier-than-thou attitude by any Christian group or by the Christian movement as such. With few exceptions, Christians and Christian groups have come to terms with the world. Let us frankly admit in sackcloth and ashes that "the de-Christianisation characteristic of the modern age is, to a large extent, the product of the infidelity of the Christians to their own faith." [30]

Another phase of Christianity's inner renewal is a strengthening of institutional religion. Trueblood in several places emphasizes this matter. He suggests that a strictly individual religion may do fairly well in times of prosperity but that something stronger is needed in a time of genuine crisis. He adds, "Our civilization cannot be rebuilt unless institutional religion is revived and loyally supported." [31] He further says: "The sober fact is that the Christian churches and the Hebrew synagogues are the only organizations in our civilization whose *primary* purpose is to keep alive the moral and spiritual principles without which a

[28] Berdyaev, Towards a New Epoch, p. 52.
[29] Ibid., p. 49.
[30] Brunner, Christianity and Civilization, Part I, p. 11.
[31] Foundations of Reconstruction, p. 43.

decent world is impossible." [32] This means that "prophets of the half-way house," such as Lewis Mumford, may be keen in their insight into the nature of the contemporary crisis and may be correct when they insist on the need for repentance and spiritual renewal, but they largely nullify what good they would do otherwise when they refuse to identify themselves with institutionalized religion. The renewal that is needed is a renewal within the lives of individual Christians, but also within the existing forms of organized Christianity.

The Christian church more than once has found spiritual renewal in the past by returning to the religion of Jesus, by catching again the spirit of his life, and by understanding a little better the simplicity and depth of the principles that he taught. "When the Christian Religion is unable to return to Jesus in order to go forward with the spirit of Jesus it will be a sure sign that Christianity has reached decrepitude and that its dissolution is imminent. To go back to the point in the road where you took the wrong turning, . . . is neither reactionary nor unnecessary if you would reach your destination." [33]

If organized Christianity catches again the spirit of the life and teachings of Jesus, it will recover the faith it so largely has lost in God, in his power, and in his ultimate triumph in the world. It will recapture a deep sense of divine mission and the power and purpose to proclaim the gospel undiluted, with the conviction that it will not return void but that it is the only hope for the individual and the world.

A revival of Christian faith also will mean the recovery of moral conviction and Christian courage. Such a recovery

[32] *Ibid.*, p. 50.
[33] H. D. A. Major, *Civilization and Religious Values* (London: George Allen and Unwin, Ltd., 1948), p. 73.

will give a renewal of the spirit of martyrdom that has characterized Christianity in its times of greatest triumph. Berdyaev, in speaking of modern Christians, says, "Christians have shown themselves to be less capable of sacrifice than revolutionaries, particularly the Russian revolutionaries of the nineteenth century." [34]

A return to the spirit and teachings of Jesus also will provide the basis for a reinterpretation of Christian individualism. Most of the modern movements that challenge our way of life have arisen, to some degree, as a reaction to a one-sided emphasis on the rights of the individual. The emphasis has been too exclusively on the rights of the individual and not enough on his responsibilities. Also, the emphasis has been too largely on one's own rights rather than on the rights of others. Modern individualism has been too self-centered.

Also, it should be remembered that human institutions and the social order as such have some rights as well as responsibilities. It should be remembered also that the individual becomes a person only through association with other persons. Berdyaev suggests that "only a Christian Renaissance uniting the principle of personality with that of community is capable of assuring victory over the depersonalization and dehumanization now menacing the world." [35]

Jesus taught that man finds life, real life or life on the highest level, by losing his life.[36] Paul said, "For ye, brethren, were called for freedom; only use not your freedom for an occasion to the flesh, but through love be servants one to another." [37] The freedom the Christian has in Christ is

[34] Op. cit., p. 32.
[35] Ibid., p. 70.
[36] Matt. 16:25.
[37] Gal. 5:13 ASV.

to be surrendered voluntarily for the sake of others. This is the spirit of self-denial and self-sacrifice symbolized by the cross. The way of the cross is the way of salvation, not only for the individual but also for the world. It is the way to find life; it is also the way to give life.

Another element must also enter into the renewal of contemporary Christianity if it is to be an effective instrument in the saving of civilization. The church must recover and maintain a proper balance between its divine and human natures. It must recognize that "the Church always stands in a double relationship to history, and it neglects either aspect of its existence at its peril." [38] As a human institution, the church stands within history. As a divine institution, it transcends history. In its institutional life it is largely human. In its message and mission it is divine.

Christian groups frequently have emphasized too exclusively either the human or the divine nature of the church. Those who have emphasized too exclusively the church as a human institution have tended to identify that institution with the accepted cultural patterns. But "if religion is too deeply committed to a particular cultural synthesis, it fails to maintain its transcendent character." [39] The tragedy is that when the church loses a proper sense of its divine mission, it also loses its power to lift the world toward the transcendent God, who alone is able to save that world. The Christian movement must be free from the darkness of the world if it is to dispel that darkness. When the human nature of the church is too exclusively stressed, there is a tendency to tone down or to dilute the Christian message to such a degree that it loses its ability to challenge the world.

[38] Charles D. Kean, *Christianity and the Cultural Crisis* (New York: The Association Press, 1944), p. 193.

[39] Christopher Dawson, *Religion and Culture* (New York: Sheed and Ward, 1948), p. 196.

"On the other hand, if religion attempts to emancipate itself completely from its bond with culture, it makes for the secularization of culture." [40] This is the temptation of those who think too largely of the church as a divine institution. They tend to be indifferent to the world and to separate themselves so far as possible from the world. When carried to the extreme, this means the loss of any effective Christian influence on the world.

What is needed within the Christian movement is a working synthesis of a conservative theology with a progressive attitude toward the application of the gospel to every area of life. Only a religion that joins together a deep consciousness of sin and of man's inability to save himself and his world, with a strong faith in God's ability to save not only individuals but the world, will be found adequate for our day.

INTERVENTION OF GOD

We have suggested that men and civilizations must return to God if they are to be saved. We have suggested also that even organized Christianity must return to the first principles of the Christian movement. While we as individuals should do everything we can to encourage such a return to God, we should recognize that only God can give the renewal that is needed. God alone can forgive our sins and create within us the insight and provide for us the resources for the renewal of civilization.

The God revealed in the Bible is not only "our Father," but he is also the God of the nations. We can be sure that he not only was, but that he is, the most creative and dynamic force in history.

[40] *Ibid.*, p. 196.

History reveals that God at times steps into the historical process in unusual ways. There are evidences that he sets limits beyond which he will not permit nations and civilizations to go. His intervention in the affairs of a nation or a civilization may take the form of a judgment against that nation or civilization. It should be remembered, however, that God's judgments will be redemptive if men and nations will co-operate with him. The prophets of God, in the Old Testament and since, have frequently announced the coming judgment of God, but in the same breath they have always proclaimed a message of hope.

Some may brush such a view aside as an apocalyptic conception of history. If by the apocalyptic view of history one means the intervention of God in history, then history itself proves the validity of the concept. The biblical record reveals that God actively participated not only in the life of Israel but also in the affairs of other nations. What he did then, he has continued to do through the centuries. He has been a factor in the rise and the fall of nations and civilizations.

God's participation in the affairs of nations and civilizations is not on an arbitrary basis. He has established the basic laws of life not only for individuals but also for society and for the institutions of society. These laws set the limits for men and society and carry their own penalties. The penalties are not exterior to the laws; they are inherent in the laws. Nations and civilizations, as well as individuals, cannot indefinitely violate God's laws without reaping the consequences. The "consequences" represent the judgment of God. This means that the judgment of God is not the act of an arbitrary Oriental despot but the act of a God of law and order. This does not mean that God may not step into life in unusual ways. Ordinarily, however, God works through the orderly processes of the basic laws of life—laws which are divine in their origin.

At times in the past God has been active to an unusual degree in the life of nations and civilizations. Such was true in the days of the Renaissance and the Reformation, of the Wesley revival in England, and of the Great Awakening in America. Let us not forget that these movements were not exclusively religious revivals. They were important elements in the reshaping of economic and political life.

If we believe in a God who has been, and is, a creative force in the world, then prayer for the world and its problems should be an important phase of the total Christian strategy. We should talk to our Heavenly Father, who is the sovereign God, not only about our immediate personal needs, but we should also talk to him about the problems of our nation and of our world. A period of serious crisis such as the present one is no time for a little or a limited God. We need a strong, confident faith that God can do something about the world situation.

Let us never forget that times of crisis have frequently been times when God gave to the world a new revelation of himself and of his power and will. Let us keep alert for new insights from him.

Let us also remember that a time of crisis demands a new demonstration of the true Christian spirit. God will do his part to cure the ills of our world. Will we do our part by devoting ourselves unselfishly to the fulfilment of his will for us in the world? As we give ourselves in service in co-operation with the Holy Spirit, let us not forget that we serve a sovereign, triumphant God. He may seem to lose some battles, but he will win the war against evil. He will have the last word.

7

A PERSONAL PROGRAM

WHAT can we do concerning the present world situation? Can an individual do anything of real significance? Will not one's best efforts be of little importance compared to the problems of the world?

A little reflection may reveal that we hold within our grasp the only resources that can be of any permanent value in solving the world crisis. The crisis is basically spiritual; the cure must be spiritual. If the cure is to be spiritual, then spiritual means or methods must be used. We should remember that the resources of the eternal, sovereign God are available to us and to all his children.

The following brief statements suggest some things all of us can do:

1. We can keep informed and alert concerning political, economic, and religious movements in the world.

2. We can re-examine our own personal Christian experience. Unless we have had a vital experience with the living Christ which makes us new creatures in Christ Jesus,

we shall not have the inner resources to meet the challenge of the contemporary period.

3. We can broaden our conception of what it means to be a real Christian and also help others to understand that the Christian religion is as broad as life itself, and that being a good Christian means being a Christian in every relation of life.

4. We can purpose in our hearts that we will not be satisfied to be average, nominal, or mediocre Christians, but that we shall strive to be maximum Christians for Christ.

5. We can recognize that, regardless of our vocation or profession, our chief business as children of God is to promote his cause and kingdom among men.

6. We can place supreme value on things spiritual rather than on things material, considering the latter primarily as instruments or means through which the spiritual may be promoted.

7. We can take some time each day for a period of quiet waiting before the Lord, asking him and expecting him to reveal his will and way to us. This period may and should include Bible study, prayer, and meditation.

8. We can pray, individually and as a family group, not only for ourselves, our loved ones, our church, and our denomination, but also for our nation, our world, and our civilization. We can pray with an abiding faith that our God is mighty enough and big enough to do something about the problems of our world.

9. We can open our hearts and every area of our lives to the leadership of the Spirit of God, seeking as best we can to dedicate our lives to God and to the doing of his will.

10. We can be broad in our vision, our sympathies, and our perspective. We can carry a world in our hearts.

11. We can open our eyes to the critical situation in the world and pass on to others something of our sense of urgency.

12. We can remember that the commission that Christ gave to his disciples has never been repealed, and that the failure of Christians to be as missionary-minded as they should have been has been an important factor in creating the contemporary crisis.

13. We can do what we can to help our churches to lift up their eyes and to look on the fields that are white unto harvest. We can challenge our churches to share more generously with our missionary agencies that the good news of Christ may be carried to all men of all nations. We also can challenge our young people to dedicate themselves to a life of unselfish service and to devote their talents and time to the promotion of the cause of Christ among men.

14. We can strike a match. This was the advice recently given to some college young people, who wanted to know what they could do. They were reminded that when all the lights in a giant stadium were out, the striking of one match was clearly visible throughout the entire stadium. The darkness around us is deep enough that even the striking of one match will be noticeable. There is also a possibility that the striking of one match might encourage others to strike their matches. Thus enough light may be generated to make an impact on the world.

Let us put into practice more than a mere program and have more than a superficial purpose. Let us make it a life commitment, a committal that will match in devotion the Christian martyrs of the past and the revolutionaries of the present.